## Praise for *Shifting: How School Leaders Can Create a Culture of Change*

"Books on change tend to be either slickly glib and useless, or hopelessly complex and useless. *Shifting* offers a path that weaves together theory and stories from the front line, models, and a practical call to action. It's an essential primer for change, whether you work in education or not."

**—Michael Bungay Stanier**
Author, *The Coaching Habit*

"Knowing when and how to launch a change initiative is often as challenging as knowing when and how to hop onto a swinging jump rope. The process can be quite daunting. *Shifting* provides easy-to-manage examples of how leadership must enact change with intentionality and build guideposts that staff can utilize when navigating the complex variables of who, what, when, and why in organizational transformation. The authors lead the reader to understand that change is never simply a single initiative or series of events, rather it is a multifaceted process that involves shifting the mindset of the whole. The paradigm shift changes you from the inside out. Powerful . . ."

**—Gayle Stinson**
Superintendent of Schools, Lake Dallas ISD
Past President, TASA

"*Shifting: How School Leaders Can Create a Culture of Change* could be a breakthrough book on change management in education. The authors have done a masterful job of combining theory and practice for the reader. The special sauce is the quotes and stories of the practitioners throughout each chapter. The book comes alive to the point that it feels like you are in conversation and learning from the authors and leaders who are sharing their knowledge. Every leader needs to read this book before they embark on change to choose the best strategies and to understand their role in the change process."

**—Lyle Kirtman**
CEO, Future Management Systems
Author, *Coherent School Leadership: Forging Clarity From Complexity* with Michael Fullan

"At last, a book on how to lead productive change that embodies the premise that educational leaders should model what we want to see in the classroom. We can trust *Shifting: How School Leaders Can Create a Culture of Change* because it is filled with case studies about working educators from a variety of backgrounds. Reflective prompts guide teachers and administrators to adapt these insights to their unique school settings. *Shifting* speaks with an authentic voice and delivers the strategies that help us consider the changes we want so as to develop the schools we need."

**—Peter Pappas**
Developer of the "Taxonomy of Reflection"
University of Portland—School of Education

"As someone who knows first-hand how challenging it is to lead and sustain long-term, transformational change, I am especially grateful for this book. The authors condense insights from decades of research and dozens of frontline change leaders to extend a supportive hand to every educator who wants and needs to lead change, but doesn't know where to begin. My advice to every educator: keep this book close. If you don't have the answers now, this book gives you the right questions and invaluable "real world" gold nugget guidance—and that will be enough."

**—April Armstrong**
CEO, AHA Insight

"A must-read for aspiring or current education practitioners, and highly recommended for leaders of organizations experiencing a culture of constant flux and change. In a time when "self" seems to eclipse "team," the authors remind us that people are at the center of any effective change, and leaders who demonstrate integrity, vulnerability, intentionality and mindfulness are far more likely to achieve organizational outcomes that have a lasting impact on all children."

**—Lynne B. Pierson**
Former Connecticut Superintendent of Schools

"We love *Shifting* because the authors are candid about what schools need to do to "shift" toward excellence. Too many change initiatives fail because of surface-level actions and a focus on *what we're doing* instead of actually *getting results*. This book confronts that reality in an honest way, but also provides a call-to-action with exactly what leaders need to do next. The "Try This" sections are perfect—providing both a platform for reflection and the critical steps forward."

—**Joseph Jones** and **T.J. Vari**
Authors, *Candid and Compassionate Feedback: Transforming Everyday Practice in Schools*

# Shifting

# Shifting

## How School Leaders Can Create a Culture of Change

Kirsten Richert

Jeffrey Ikler

Margaret Zacchei

*Foreword by Kimberly Davis*

**FOR INFORMATION:**

Corwin

A SAGE Company

2455 Teller Road

Thousand Oaks, California 91320

(800) 233-9936

www.corwin.com

SAGE Publications Ltd.

1 Oliver's Yard

55 City Road

London EC1Y 1SP

United Kingdom

SAGE Publications India Pvt. Ltd.

B 1/I 1 Mohan Cooperative Industrial Area

Mathura Road, New Delhi 110 044

India

SAGE Publications Asia-Pacific Pte. Ltd.

18 Cross Street #10-10/11/12

China Square Central

Singapore 048423

Publisher: Arnis Burvikovs

Acquisitions Editor: Ariel Curry

Development Editor: Desirée A. Bartlett

Associate Editor: Eliza B. Erickson

Project Editor: Amy Schroller

Copy Editor: Jared Leighton

Typesetter: Hurix Digital

Proofreader: Theresa Kay

Indexer: Molly Hall

Cover Designer: Gail Buschman

Marketing Manager: Sharon Pendergast

Printed in the United States of America

*Library of Congress Cataloging-in-Publication Data*

Names: Richert, Kirsten, author. | Ikler, Jeff, author. | Zacchei, Margaret, author.

Title: Shifting : how school leaders can create a culture of change / Kirsten Richert, Jeff Ikler, Margaret Zacchei.

Description: First edition. | Thousand Oaks, California : Corwin Press, [2020] | Includes bibliographical references.

Identifiers: LCCN 2019047184 | ISBN 9781544381398 (paperback) | ISBN 9781544381374 (epub) | ISBN 9781544381367 (epub) | ISBN 9781544381381 (ebook)

Subjects: LCSH: Educational leadership. | Educational change. | Education—Aims and objectives.

Classification: LCC LB2806 .I37 2020 | DDC 371.2—dc23

LC record available at https://lccn.loc.gov/2019047184

ISBN 978-1-5443-8139-8

This book is printed on acid-free paper.

SUSTAINABLE FORESTRY INITIATIVE

Certified Chain of Custody
Promoting Sustainable Forestry
www.sfiprogram.org
SFI-01268

20 21 22 23 24 10 9 8 7 6 5 4 3 2 1

# Contents

# Website Table
# of Contents

online resources

Scan this QR code or visit the website at
www.shiftingforimpact.com
to access the links listed above.

# Foreword

As I was leaning over my teenage son's shoulder, oohing and ahh-ing over the graphic design project that he had just pulled up from Google Docs, I couldn't help but shake my head in wonder. How much has changed since I was a student! My son's world is completely different. His texts are all online. He collaborates with his classmates, sharing files that are stored in the cloud. His assignments live on a portal. For goodness sake, he's been using PowerPoint since he was in the third grade!

Given the fact that when I graduated from high school, I was beyond thrilled to get a Smith Corona Coronamatic 2500 Electric Typewriter, it's hard to wrap my head around what I'm seeing. So much has changed in such a short amount of time, and the pace is only getting faster. According to futurist Jim Carroll, "Sixty-five percent of the children who are in pre-school today will work in a job or career that doesn't yet exist." And "half of what students learn in their first year at college is obsolete or revised—by the time they graduate." Today's children need to be prepared for a future that lies beyond my imagination, and their springboard, our schools, must heed the call.

The inescapable truth is that you, as educators, are caught in the over-whelming reality that you must not only *understand* the shifting needs of today's world but, simultaneously, *create* learning environments that equip students for tomorrow's world.

You must become masterful changemakers.

What I know to be true is that you got into education because you care. You care about students. You care about your communities. You care about improving student performance, preparing them for the future as if it were today. You care about making a difference. But far too often, good teachers and talented administrators find them-selves frustrated, demoralized, and burnt out by a plethora of new initiatives, standardized tests, and mandated curriculums. You're left feeling unsupported and uninspired and sometimes forgetting why you're doing what you're doing in the first place. It's no wonder, when the demand for change rears its ugly head, that the last thing you want to do is to give it a parade.

But what if you could bring that kind of enthusiasm to improve today and embrace the future?

What if you could harness that kind of energy in your staff and collectively bring your best to make a lasting impact on the lives of your students?

What if the process of change could create a more positive, engaged, and fulfilling workplace?

What if, collectively, you could ignite a sense of purpose and pride in one another and unite your team around a shared vision?

*Shifting: How School Leaders Can Create a Culture of Change* makes this possible. The authors, with their long, rich educational backgrounds, wrote this book not only to help school leaders and their faculty proactively and coherently navigate unprecedented change on behalf of students and teachers but also to cultivate a healthy work environment where changemakers can thrive. They have written a book that uniquely weaves together the voices of experienced educators and transformational leadership and organizational practices, making it possible for educational change leaders—you—to achieve desired outcomes and have the impact they envision. As a parent and educator-advocate, I can't think of a better seed for tomorrow.

Kimberly Davis
Author, *Brave Leadership*

# Acknowledgments

*"If I have seen a little further, it is by standing on the shoulders of giants."*

— Isaac Newton in a letter to his rival,
Robert Hooke, in 1676

Few, if any, works of nonfiction are the products of the author's mind alone. This book is no exception. We are extremely grateful for the contributions we received from so many individuals. Their wisdom, advice, and support were invaluable.

First, we want to thank the various school leaders we interviewed— many more than once—whose experiences and insight richly informed and reinforced our own thinking. A book on leading effective change in schools would be an empty vessel without their insights.

Jonathan Adams, assistant principal for teaching and learning, International School of Luxembourg

Anita Clay, retired teacher, author, literacy consultant, St. Louis, Missouri

Adam Dovico, principal, Moore Magnet Elementary School, Winston-Salem, North Carolina

Diane Dugas, director of talent management, EASTCONN Education, Univeristy of Connecticut

Greg Ewing, superintendent, Las Cruces Public Schools, New Mexico

Richard Gonzales, director, Educational Leader Preparation Programs, NEAG School of Education, Univeristy of Connecticut

Deb Gustafson, executive director of student services, USD 475, Junction City, Kansas; formerly principal, Ware Elementary School, Fort Riley, Kansas

Mary Howard, nationally known literacy specialist; author (*Good to Great Teaching, RTI From All Sides, Moving Forward With RTI*), Tulsa, Oklahoma

Tom Marshall, principal, Stony Lane Elementary School, Paramus, New Jersey

Fran McVeigh, literacy consultant, former principal and professional development coordinator, Ottumwa, Iowa

Peter McWain, director of curriculum and instruction, Santa Fe Public Schools, New Mexico

Kristy Moody, principal, Fairmount Park Elementary School, St. Petersburg, Florida

Todd Nesloney, principal, Webb Elementary School, Navasota, Texas

Michael Oliver, principal, Zaharis Elementary School, Mesa, Arizona

Danny Papa, K–12 supervisor of social studies, fine arts, and technology education, Jefferson Township Public Schools, New Jersey

Evan Robb, principal, Johnson Williams Middle School, Berryville, Virginia

Laura Robb, retired teacher, literacy consultant, Clarke County, Virginia

Karen Rue, clinical professor of K–12 educational leadership at Baylor University and former superintendent, Northwest ISD, Texas

Donna Schilke, former principal, Smith Middle School, Glastonbury, Connecticut

Dave Schuler, superintendent, Arlington Heights Public Schools, Arizona

Steven Stone, superintendent, Dracut Public Schools, Massachusetts

Patrick Sweeney, learning consultant, Pivot Learning; former superintendent, Napa Valley Schools, California

Lamarr Thomas, principal, Janis E. Dismus Middle School, Englewood, New Jersey

Ivette Visbal, dean of students at New Vista High School, Boulder, Colorado

Rona Wilensky, director of mindfulness programs, PassageWorks Institute, Denver, Colorado

Next, there is a group of thought leaders from whom we drew critical direction and support. They are Courtney Ackerman, Donna Anderson Davis, Michael Bungay Stanier, Shelley Brown, Michael Bunting, Kimberly Davis, Sarah Elkins, Oksana Esberard, Melissa Hughes, Lyle Kirtman, Amnon Levav, Mark Mitrovich, Steve Paul, Ani Steele, and Heather Younger. All are tireless rock stars in support of education in the broadest sense of the term.

We are indebted to our colleagues at Corwin who provided guidance to all of our "Now, how do we handle . . . ?" inquiries. They are Eliza Erickson, Desirée Bartlett, Sharon Pendergast, Amy Schroller, Ariel Curry, and Arnis Burvikovs. It was Arnis who responded to our original proposal with "I like the idea. Let's take it to the next step."

Lastly, no acknowledgments would be complete without mentioning the special cheerleaders, hand-holders, and door-openers in our lives. We collectively kneel for Jennifer, Esmilda, and David.

## Publisher's Acknowledgments

Corwin gratefully acknowledges the contributions of the following reviewers:

Helene Alalouf, educational consultant, New York, NY

Roseanne Lopez, associate superintendent for elementary education, Tucson, AZ

Neil MacNeill, head master, Independent Primary School, Ellenbrook, Western Australia

Keith T. Myatt, retired professor, Graduate School Leadership Programs, Carson, CA

LaQuita Outlaw, principal, Grades 6–8, Bay Shore, NY

Lena Marie Rockwood, high school assistant principal, Revere, MA

# About the Authors

**Kirsten Richert** is an innovation expert who works with leaders on transformational efforts. Kirsten teaches design thinking, communication, and innovation at a number of colleges in the greater NYC area. Her teaching draws upon her experience in three core disciplines: business management, ideation methodology, and facilitation.

She received her undergraduate degree in social science from Hampshire College, her master's degree in social studies education from Teachers College at Columbia University, and her training in innovation and facilitation methods from SIT (Systematic Inventive Thinking) and ToP (Technology of Participation).

Formerly vice president of product management and marketing at Pearson, the world's leading educational publisher, Kirsten oversaw the creation of breakthrough "digital-first" K–12 curriculum. Trained as a corporate on-call innovation coach, she's helped teams plan new efforts, generate ideas, and execute on strategies.

Now, as an innovation catalyst, Kirsten guides change efforts for organizations, especially in the areas of education and human development. She is particularly interested in organizations that integrate the arts into their work toward social change, such as the Alliance for Arts and Health New Jersey, Real Beauty: Uncovered, and The Barat Foundation.

 **Jeffrey (Jeff) Ikler** is director of Quetico Career and Leadership Coaching, a firm dedicated to helping individuals overcome career issues and leaders develop sustained changes in their leadership practices and organizations. He received his certificate in coaching from the Coach Training Institute, a firm recognized as one of the leading coach-training organizations in the world. His approach blends data-driven coaching and consulting informed by working for more than thirty-five years in the corporate world.

Jeff holds a master's in the teaching of history, along with a bachelor's in history, from the University of Illinois. He taught high school history in Maywood and Batavia, Illinois, for seven years. Like Kirsten, he is a certified innovation facilitator using the SIT (systematic inventive thinking) process.

He is a former executive vice president at Pearson Learning where he directed the development of text- and technology-based products for all disciplines. He finished his career at Pearson by leading the development of its multidimensional Leadership Development program for school administrators, working closely with authors Lyle Kirtman and Michael Fullan. He currently works with Lyle Kirtman to support change in school districts and nonprofit organizations.

Jeff and Kirsten also cohost *Getting Unstuck—Shift for Impact*, a podcast that helps individuals and organizations identify and overcome obstacles that stand in the way of implementing changes that lead toward achieving desired results and impact.

**Margaret Zacchei** is an innovative educational leader and consultant with twenty-five years of experience as an elementary principal and teacher. Through Margaret's leadership and engagement of staff, the school where she was principal until 2017 received the highest recognition for achievement by the Connecticut Department of Education in 2015–2016 and 2016–2017.

Margaret's leadership style can be summarized in three words: collaboration, communication, and community. Throughout her career, she has engaged teachers, students, parents, and fellow administrators to collaboratively define problems and implement practical solutions that achieve sustainable school improvement.

Margaret is currently serving as a consultant and coach to school districts and administrations, sharing her experiences and perspective as a leader and change agent to help them achieve their goals. She is also coaching aspiring leaders enrolled in the University of Connecticut's administrator preparation program as they complete a two-year internship program in various districts in the state.

# Preface

*"Change is good. You go first."*

—Dilbert (Adams, 2005)

The topic of change has been studied and turned over and studied again with good reason: change can be beneficial, but changing is hard. The human brain—and its leadership and organizational manifestations—is wired for certainty and to maintain the status quo. Going all the way back to our human roots, there is potential danger in stepping away from the warmth and light of our campfire, however curious we are with what might lie beyond it.

But there is also incredible potential in getting change right. By the time you read this passage, the nation will have celebrated the fiftieth anniversary of the Apollo 11 moon landing. The Apollo program was the single largest enterprise ever undertaken by man, dwarfing the building of the pyramids, the Panama Canal, or our interstate highway system. It involved some 420,000 scientists, engineers, technicians, electricians, and just about any other type of "cians" you can imagine. And it required some two thousand contractors and subcontractors to work together to put the complicated Apollo puzzle together piece by piece.

President Kennedy may have laid down the challenge to the nation to "commit itself to achieving the goal, before this decade is out, of landing a man on the moon and returning him safely to the Earth," but as anyone on the project would tell you, knowing *how* to go to the moon was an entirely different matter.

The team simply didn't know what it didn't know.

In the early sixties, a rocket that was powerful enough to get astronauts to the moon didn't exist. Nor was there an agreed-upon system to get them *on* and *off* the moon.

Computers, which were going to be the single most critical component of navigating in space, were, at the time, the size of a large refrigerator or walk-in closets. Imagine that inside what we know today as the tiny confines of the Apollo Command Module.

No one knew how to undock, dock, and redock two spacecraft in space. Solving that problem became a key determinant of success.

Mathematics certainly existed, but the extremely complicated math formulas required to determine flight paths, orbits, and docking maneuvers didn't.

Oh, those pesky details.

The collective effort overcame innumerable hurdles and setbacks, including the deaths of three astronauts. It required massive changes in computing, rocketry, organizational management, problem solving, and attitudes. Fundamentally, it required everyone to remain insanely curious, to experiment to find out what worked, and to learn that what has never been done before didn't mean it can't be done now.

We know how the story ends. Change can be very, very worth it.

## Why This Book on Change?

This is a book about shifting how you lead productive, desired change in schools. And when we say *change*, we're referring to *complex* changes such as implementing a block schedule, adopting new instructional strategies, or changing the school culture to achieve desired outcomes. These are the types of changes that can take many months or years to complete depending on a variety of factors. That said, the points we make herein can also positively impact the day-to-day adjustments that you must make in what is often the hyperactive school or district setting.

## Shifting Traditional Thinking About School Change

This book shifts traditional thinking about change in schools in three important ways:

- It *shifts* from what can often be an understandably tactical reaction to outside influences and influencers to one of purposeful changes in support of a school or district's *why*—the overall impact either seeks to have relative to those it serves.

- It *shifts* from what can be a weighted focus on the technical and management aspects of change to a more balanced explanation that emphasizes a focus on the people leading and implementing the change. As such, we're as much interested in the neuroscience of change as we are in the mechanical process of change.

*Shifting*, in its heart and soul, is a book about school leadership and its relationship to and impact on the organization. *Shifting* is a move away from the top-down, command-and-control type of leadership to one where leaders seek to develop their own curiosity, vulnerability, and authenticity, all in the service of meaningful collaboration.

- It *shifts* from a mindset that change is a series of singular, disconnected, reactive events to one where change actions are proactively engaged in and looked at as cohesively working toward desired outcomes and impact.

## Figure 0.1  Three Essential Shifts to Create Productive Change

Less of ...                                          More of ...

Disconnected reactions to outside influences → **1** → Sustained, proactive responses focused on the organizational why

A focus on the mechanics → **2** → A focus on the people leading and implementing change

A top-down, command-and-control approach → **3** → Shared leadership and meaningful collaboration

Ultimately, this is a book about promoting a culture that produces productive change on behalf of the population the school or district serves—a culture promoted through an atmosphere of curiosity, experimentation, and sustained learning. According to Dave Schuler, 2018 Illinois and National Superintendent of the Year, with whom we spoke in preparation for writing this book, the *sustained learning* part takes faculty members back to why they got into education in the first place. "I think there's a huge misnomer that teachers get into teaching because they love to teach. I think teachers get into teaching because they love to learn."

## Five Distinguishing Hallmarks

Five elements distinguish our approach.

### Element 1: The ARC Model of Change

Books that outline a framework or process for change do so because it provides a pathway with handrails: Now you are here. We fully support that notion but wanted to create a process that was infinitely simple to understand and negotiate without being simplistic. Our process is linear—we start here, move here, and so on—but it's not a straight line. It can and must circle back on itself when the underlying elements of change require it.

So we created the ARC model of change, shown in Figure 0.2, running parallel to the other work the school and or district must manage—both pathways contributing to the impact the school or district is trying to have on behalf of the students and community it serves. This illustration shows a single, complex change underway. In Chapter 9, we present a more complex—and perhaps more realistic—model showing multiple changes underway simultaneously.

We're often asked, "How long does any single change take?" That's an extremely complicated question to answer because there are so many variables. A quick win might be accomplished in a few months while some complex change efforts, as some of our interviewees suggested, could take years. One consistent piece of advice we received from the educators who we interviewed for the book was "Go slow to go fast." As we will discuss in the chapters ahead, the urgency of change is around the imperative to address the issue, not the pace at which you do so. Be curious. Experiment. Learn.

## Figure 0.2   The ARC Model of Change

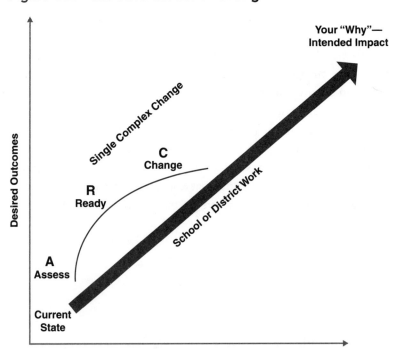

**A = *Assess*** allows you to take stock of your situation—including yourself, your organization, and your environment—so you can better understand the full picture and then clearly define what impact you intend to have and what problem you are trying to solve with a specific change.

**R = *Ready*** helps you and your team prepare to make a change by focusing on the problem; coming up with many potential solutions; considering them given time, resources, and impact; and choosing how you will proceed.

**C = *Change*** gets you into motion, experimenting by taking action and monitoring progress during and after the change. *Change* asks you to evaluate early results, refine your actions, build momentum, acknowledge wins, and keep your energy up until you have completely implemented the solution.

We will fully explore each of these phases in the pages that follow.

### Element 2: Leadership Spotlights

Throughout the book, you will see **Leadership Spotlights**—sidebars in the manuscript that highlight essential leadership insights to guide you in implementing change in your schools.

### Element 3: Minds-On, Hands-On Approach

Sometimes reading about a topic isn't enough, so in addition to the numerous embedded questions throughout the narrative, we've built in **Try This** activities at the end of every chapter to help shape your skills, thinking, and experimentation.

In addition, you'll encounter references throughout to additional online activities, models, and worked-out examples, which can be found at www.shiftingforimpact.com. As important as they are, we felt including these tools directly in the narrative would have interrupted the flow.

### Element 4: Insights From Change Leaders

Because of our focus on the importance of people in the change process, we wanted to hear periodically from leaders who are wrestling with the real issues of change. So we conducted extensive interviews and included their stories at key junctures to make or reinforce a point in the narrative. They show up as

- brief quotes—a sentence or two,
- **Leader Stories**—sixteen lengthier comments that provide deeper insight, and

- **Leader Voices**—seventeen brief recordings accessed via the QR code located on page xiv as well as at the end of each chapter, or found at the book's website, www.shiftingforimpact.com.

### Element 5: An Integrated Tapestry of Wisdom

Professional support books are often defined by their narrow focus: You read one for one purpose and another for a different purpose. One of the things we've attempted to do here is to weave the wisdom from a number of sources together to form a new tapestry around the topics of leadership and change, including our ARC model of change. The experienced educators among you may meet some old friends, such as Jim Collins, Daniel Goleman, and Liz Wiseman, but we're also bringing forth voices that may be new to you, such as Kimberly Davis's (2018) *Brave Leadership*, Patrick Lencioni's (2012) *The Advantage*, and Michael Bungay Stanier's (2016) *The Coaching Habit*. It's our intent to weave these voices together in a unique cloth that enriches your reading experience and your ability to undertake purposeful change through our ARC model.

## Who Is This Book Intended For?

We started out writing this book for school administrators, but as we worked through it, we became convinced the message could serve the entire school staff, and here's why. As you'll read within, we believe that when you consider a complex change process in education, you should be asking yourself *and* the larger organization some key questions:

*Why are we considering this change?*

*How does this change tie into other change initiatives we have underway or have implemented?*

*What outcomes and overall impact are we trying to achieve on behalf of those we serve?*

Simply put, effective change doesn't happen because of one person. It's the *we* that undertakes change and makes it succeed. *Shifting* could easily be used for a book study by a team in advance of tackling a complex change.

That said, changing how you change ultimately starts with you. It's only a short step from the previous questions to some fundamental ones that reflect back on an earlier you—the you who stepped into a classroom or administrative office for the first time:

*Why did I get involved in education to begin with?*

*What was I trying to accomplish for my students and for myself?*

*What impact was I trying to have?*

Pausing to reflect on those questions is the first step toward becoming the change leader you want and need to be.

Those individuals you have wanted to serve since day one are waiting.

Kirsten Richert

Jeff Ikler

Margaret Zacchei
*Forest Hills, New York*
*2019*

# Shifting

## A New Way to Look at Change

# 1

Avoiding change failure starts with building and getting a commitment to an organizational why—the core belief underlying what the district and/or school is attempting to accomplish on behalf of those it serves.

**THE BIG SHIFT**

## A LEADER'S STORY

"It was a miserable fail."

Dr. Karen Rue, former superintendent
Northwest ISD, Texas
**Now, Clinical Professor, K–12 Educational Leadership,**
**Baylor University**

In my first year in the district, I just shoved things down people's throats. I got there and evaluated the elementary reading program and realized there was something missing. I knew exactly what needed to happen, so I told people what needed to happen. I wanted them to begin with staff development on what a balanced reading program was. They'd never had that kind of PD. They also didn't understand all the program components, so I wanted to bring in professional development to address those two issues. What I didn't do was let people discover the issues themselves. I didn't set the stage. I didn't give them the time to do their own learning. I didn't start with a small ask, such as, "Would the principals get together with your key reading people at your elementary levels, with whomever, study what a balanced reading program is, and look at it in light of our own and make some recommendations about what we might need?" I can think

(Continued)

(Continued) of a hundred ways I could've done it differently, but I didn't. I came in as the expert. I knew what we needed. I went about putting it in place.

And it was sabotaged. People went through the motions, but they never did it. I remember telling one of the people I worked with, "I'm smarter than this. I should've known this." It was a miserable fail.

## Why Change Initiatives Fail

According to the Gallup Organization, upwards of 70 percent of all complex change initiatives fail annually (Leonard & Coltea, 2013). Interestingly, Gallup notes that roughly the *same* percentage of all U.S. employees feel disengaged from their work. Is that figure a mere coincidence (Schwantes, 2017)?

The literature is replete with stories about the one, three, five, seven, ten, or fifty reasons why proposed changes don't go as planned. Our assessment of those reasons, backed up by more than one hundred years of combined experience in business and education, has led us to focus on three, which we will examine throughout the book.

Yes, complex change initiatives also require attention to be paid to the more technical factors of skill acquisition, resources, timetables, infrastructure, and the change plan itself, but we believe that change success ultimately rests as much or more on human nature and behavior.

Many of you reading this narrative are probably familiar with the model of change that Professor Tim Knoster shared back in 1991. It's a clear and simple model of what can derail change efforts and negatively impact culture. There, Knoster showed that if certain change factors weren't addressed, the result in the organization could be confusion, sabotage, anxiety, resistance, and frustration—all *human* implications (Moesby, 2004). We can only conclude that the 70 percent of organizations that experience change

### MAKING SENSE OF IT

Words matter, and we use three terms throughout with specific meanings: *outcome*, *impact*, and *organizational why*.

***Outcome:*** The result of a single change event (e.g., As a result of revising the building schedule, teachers are now meeting and engaging in collaborative planning twice a week).

***Impact:*** The overall benefits that serve a population, such as students, as a result of a series of cohesive changes (e.g., Through effective collaborative planning and instruction around solving complex and real-world problems, students' engagement and achievement have increased).

***Organizational Why:*** The core belief underlying what impact the district and/or school seeks to have relative to those it serves (e.g., To succeed in a rapidly changing world, students need to be increasingly challenged to [1] demonstrate their ability to use their knowledge and skills in new and unrehearsed ways to solve complex, real-world problems and [2] justify their answers).

failure did not address those potential implications either adequately or accurately and, as a result, suffered a commensurate negative impact on staff.

Thus, two questions need to be thoroughly examined, which we will start to do here and then more fully examine in subsequent chapters:

- Who is leading the change effort, and do they view themselves as a *valued* leader of any change that works toward the organizational why?

- Who is executing the change effort, and do they view themselves as a *valued* contributor to the why behind the change?

The word *valued* is particularly important in both of these questions. As neuroscience researcher Dr. Melissa Hughes observed in a vlog post, "When we see ourselves as a vital part of the work, that's when our engagement grows. This is when we know that what we do really matters and that our colleagues value our contributions." In short, a major component of change success is the engagement of the people leading and executing the change (Hughes, 2019).

## "Houston, we have a problem." (Actually, we have three of them.)

Let's look at the three factors of change failure in greater depth.

## WHY CHANGE INITIATIVES FAIL

1. **Neglecting the WHY:** Failure to agree on the organizational why—the core belief underlying the overall impact the district and/or school seeks to have relative to those it serves—and to cohesively tie any changes and their desired outcomes to that *why*.

2. **Neglecting the WHO:** Failure to assess and develop the mindset, talents, and behaviors that leaders and staff need to bring about changes and their desired outcomes; to focus as much or more on the people leading and executing the change than on the specific change itself.

3. **Neglecting the WHAT:** Failure to acknowledge what people are already doing well in the school or district as it assesses conditions that speak to the need for additional change; to see change as cultural—a cohesive set of proactive actions that people undertake to serve their *why*.

When we step back and look at these three factors, our cautionary note to leaders is

*"Ignore at your peril the people charged with leading or implementing the change."*

- "Respect for self, others and community"
- "Ability to get into college"

The list went on with some duplication, and a heated discussion followed: "At the end of the day, it's about . . ."

- " . . . keeping kids secure and safe!"
- " . . . performance on high-stakes assessments because property values reflect them!"
- " . . . providing equity of opportunity!"
- " . . . ensuring that all kids have basic math and reading skills!"
- " . . . developing kids who can think and solve problems!"

It's not that any of the suggested impact statements are wrong; they're actually all important. But at the end of the day, it was clear there was no agreement on how they rolled up to a larger, more encompassing statement on the impact the district really wanted to have on behalf of its students and the community.

*The Bottom Line*—This lack of agreement on what we really want for students as the result of what we do—the *consequences* of our actions—always signals another problem: a misalignment with the instructional tools and approaches we're taking to educate them—the *curriculum* of our actions. If we don't know where we want to wind up, we're likely to be flailing, trying a little bit of this and a little bit of that to see what works. How could we expect otherwise? To paraphrase what the Cheshire Cat said to Alice: "If you don't know where you're going, any road will take you there."

## Shift 1: Change How We Look at Purpose

In 1998, Grant Wiggins and Jay McTighe introduced their Understanding by Design framework for developing curriculum. The framework was revolutionary because it sought to move educators' thinking way beyond the traditional goals and objectives they had typically included in curriculum design. Those goals and objectives, according to Wiggins and McTighe, tended to focus on the coverage of discrete facts and skills. Instead, they urged educators to begin with the end in mind and answer the questions "What outcomes are we after?" and "What do we expect students to know and do?" (Wiggins & McTighe, 2005).

Most districts implementing this approach did so at the curriculum level. But what if this approach were first applied to the district-level philosophy? One district decided to find out. The Wethersfield School District in Wethersfield, Connecticut, is located just south of Hartford and serves approximately 3,600 students. In 2019, it was ranked 43 out of 120 school districts in Connecticut and in the top 20 percent of the "Best School Districts in America" (Niche, 2019). Yet with only 67 percent of its students proficient in reading and 57 percent proficient in math, it wanted better.

*Ask a Deeper Question, Get a Deeper Answer*—Like all school districts, Wethersfield had its publicly available board mission, beliefs, and vision statements. And like it is with most school districts, these statements were a collection of well-intentioned ideas.

- Students will acquire skills and knowledge for life-long learning, enabling them to compete in a global economy and

- Be prepared to continue their education at the postsecondary level and/or to enter a viable career field of their own choosing.

- The curricula of the Wethersfield schools should be designed, implemented, and assessed to enable all students to realize their full potential.

These statements spoke to the role that schools have historically been asked to play. But what happens if you look at educating students today through the lens of the ever-changing environment that Thomas Friedman spoke of previously and away from the age-old one that Sir Ken Robinson and Evan Robb warned against?

And that's exactly what Wethersfield did. Using Simon Sinek's Golden Circle model, which explains that people buy into the emotional core behind an idea—the *why*—before they buy into the idea itself (Sinek, 2009), Wethersfield set out to answer a series of new and provocative questions:

- **Why** do we approach education the way we do?
- **How** should we educate today's learners in light of our rapidly changing world?
- **What** do we want our learners to know and be able to do *now*?

The third question was perhaps most important. Wethersfield saw that most school districts were content with being largely aspirational when they used language such as "*Students will be prepared to . . .*" The demonstration of fluency in knowledge, skill, creativity, and so on was largely something to be done at a later time. *Now* was merely about acquiring the essential foundations.

With the context of the world changing at an unprecedented rate staring the district in the face, it knew it couldn't approach instruction as it had in the past. It couldn't just focus on providing the foundations for tomorrow because tomorrow is going to be here in the next thirty minutes. Instead, the district had to define the following:

- The skills and knowledge our students need to begin to demonstrate *now* as they confront new and unrehearsed problems.
- What we expect our students to be, to know, and be able to do when they walk across the stage to receive their diplomas.
- How we can best measure student progress.

Its *why* became

> Develop students' use of 21st century skills such as problem solving and critical thinking, nurture their social and emotional character, and increase their civic awareness and behavior so they can successfully navigate in and contribute to an increasingly complex and interdependent world *now*.

In our interview, literacy specialist Mary Howard, EdD, who has worked with hundreds of districts across the country, underscores the importance of starting with the why. "When we start with the *what* and then move to the *how* [of change initiatives], we will always fall flat because we don't know what we stand for—we don't know the *why*."

Wethersfield went on to flesh out responses with board, staff, and community input in a flexible and dynamic plan of strategies and actions that will guide them over the next three to five years: *flexible* in that the document could be constantly revisited and adjusted and *dynamic* in that it is Wethersfield's attempt to be proactive about change, to create its future and the students it serves.

*The Bottom Line*—Why does starting with the why increase the likelihood of staff buying into a proposed change? In one word: neuroscience.

When leaders appeal first to the purpose and motivation behind a proposed change, they tap into the limbic system, that part of our brain that controls emotions, behaviors, memories, and arousal. When leaders tap into emotion, they increase the likelihood of establishing trust, and trust leads to supportive behavior and decision making.

School districts that have clearly defined their why—the impact they want to have on behalf of the population they serve—can look more critically at proposed changes. They can use their why as a healthy filter to ask, *Relative to everything we are already doing, how will changing in this way move us closer to achieving our desired impact?*

### Problem 2: The Who— "Leadership" Is Still Viewed as a Title, Role, and Office

Let's go back to Dr. Karen Rue's "Leader's Story" at the beginning of the chapter. Karen's reflection acknowledges her then-mistaken belief of equating her responsibility as a leader with having to control all aspects of the change initiative. It's not surprising that she would since leaders are still conditioned in a variety of ways to believe that strong leaders make bold pronouncements and take bold actions. Leaders

- are usually given special attention in terms of their office location and furniture,

- are typically positioned at the top of the organizational chart,

- have titles (e.g., principal, superintendent, department head) that convey hierarchy and status,

- traditionally assume or are de facto granted the head of the table in meetings, and

- are believed to have all the answers, and even if they don't, most are compelled to act like they do.

## MAKING SENSE OF IT

"Wait, wait, wait," you might be thinking. "Isn't the *why* just another name for mission and vision?" In our experience, no. Educational mission and vision statements tend to be

1. Expansive and inclusive—an extensive list of everything that is going on or could be going on in a district to the point that they tend to lack focus. As the old saw states, "If you stand for everything, you stand for nothing."

2. Aspirational—what students should be capable of doing after they *leave* the school, as opposed to what they should be capable of doing while *in* school.

3. Detached—they're written for the district and community; little effort, if any, is made to promote ownership and action at the individual level. (See Chapter 3: "The Why—Sharing a Clear, Agreed-Upon Purpose.")

Some of these points may seem trivial, but they reinforce the notion that leading is about authority, command, and control.

And if they are leading, others must be following.

This leader–follower paradigm becomes particularly dangerous when it comes to organizational change, and here's why. People are more likely to change if they are optimistic—feeling positive about the future. Optimism is, in part, driven by the sense of control one has, and the amount of control one feels is the result of the responsibility and ownership he or she is allowed to experience and exercise (Hecht, 2013).

Relative to change, staff who are encouraged to help shape the vision of change and the steps of its development are much more likely to commit to the change itself and feel ownership of it. Thus, the ability to influence a proposed change > drives ownership which > drives a sense of control which > drives optimism which > yields staff commitment.

### Shift 2: Change to Look at Leadership as a Set of Desired Behaviors

In *Turn the Ship Around! A True Story of Turning Followers Into Leaders*, navy captain L. David Marquet (2013) tells the story of how his life changed forever in 1998 when he received a call from his superior. He was being reassigned to take command of the USS *Santa Fe*, at the time one of the most technologically modern nuclear attack submarines in the fleet. The call was unsettling for two reasons.

For the past year, Captain Marquet had trained to take command of the submarine USS *Olympia*. He was completely familiar with every aspect of that boat and felt confident in taking over its helm of leadership. The *Santa Fe*, however, was a completely different class of submarine, one with which Captain Marquet was, technically speaking, not at all familiar. His situation was analogous to saying that an eighteen-wheeler and a pickup truck are technically both trucks. It's true, but the differences between the two are vast.

And if that weren't challenging enough, the *Santa Fe* was *the* worst-performing submarine in the U.S. Navy, and it didn't take Captain Marquet very long to figure out why. It had a major people problem, starting with its prior leadership. Captain Marquet wrote, "Leadership in the Navy, and in most organizations, is about controlling people. It divides the work into two groups of people: leaders and followers" (Marquet, 2013, p. xxv). And leaders and crew aboard the *Santa Fe* were clearly emblematic of that relationship.

*Don't Take Control, Give Control*—Leaders and followers, as a work structure, functioned well when work was mostly about giving orders and pure execution during the early days of the industrial age assembly line: "*I tell; you do.*" But in the modern, technology-heavy age we live in today, Captain Marquet posited, work demands much more cognition and metacognition on the part of the workers.

> People who are treated as followers have the expectations of followers and act like followers. As followers, they have limited decision-making authority and little incentive to give the utmost of their intellect, energy, and passion. Those who take orders usually run at half speed, underutilizing their imagination and initiative. While this doesn't matter much rowing a [an ancient Greek or Roman war galley], it's everything for operating a nuclear-powered submarine. (Marquet, 2013, p. xxvi)

It only took a couple of dramatic incidents early in his tenure aboard the *Santa Fe* for Captain Marquet to realize the extreme shortcomings of the leader–follower model and to grasp why the boat was performing so poorly. For the technically sophisticated *Santa Fe* to operate as an effective weapon of war, Captain Marquet realized that he needed 130-plus *thinkers* on board, not just order-takers. And here's the key belief underlying his model: Each member of the crew inherently had the capacity to behave differently, to give differently. They were all capable of being creative thinkers; they'd just never been asked to be.

And, thus, the leader–leader model was born. As we see in Figure 1.1 Captain Marquet and his cadre of chief petty officers had to completely shift their leadership thinking and behavior away from what was a standard command-and-control, leader–follower protocol to new leader-generating behavior.

And so, too, did the sailors aboard the *Santa Fe* have to shift. They were required to voice their thinking, supply the rationale for their actions, solve problems without being told how, and break down the silo walls that had previously isolated one department from another.

## LEADERSHIP SPOTLIGHT

Effective leaders don't direct the change; they focus on releasing the creative energy and thinking of the people who have to make the change happen. It's all about building the capacity of others.

## Figure 1.1    Select Principles of the Leader–Leader Model

| Leader–Follower: Don't Do This! | Leader–Leader: Do This! |
|---|---|
| Take control | **Give control** |
| Give orders | **Avoid giving orders** |
| Brief people | **Certify people's understanding** |
| Be questioning | **Be curious** |
| Protect information | **Share information** |
| Make inefficient processes efficient | **Cut steps and processes that don't add value** |

*Source:* Adapted from Marquet (2013, p. 205).

"I intend to _____ because _____" became a standard phrase aboard ship. In short, they had to function as *thinking* leaders within their own sphere and as part of the larger team (Marquet, 2013).

Almost immediately, Captain Marquet noted a shift. Within a year—and certainly not without growing pains—the *Santa Fe* was well on its way to becoming the most operationally proficient submarine in the *entire* U.S. Navy. And it would continue to be long after Captain Marquet's departure—all because he released the inherent genius of his crew.

*The Bottom Line*—Change leadership—really all leadership—is about anything but authority and "command and control." It's about focusing as much or more on the people responsible for the change than on the change itself. It's about unleashing staff's optimism, and to do that, leaders need to unleash staff thinking and experimentation. Leadership, then, isn't a role; it's a set of behaviors.

### Problem 3: The What—Changes Are Often Reactive Single Events, Not Proactive or Having Coherence

When we look at Figure 1.2—an undoubtedly incomplete yet lengthy list of macro changes (federal and state mandates) and micro changes (local choice and thought leader driven) initiated over the past few decades—we see the potential to look at change in education as a series of single and often disconnected constructs. We start something, do it for a time, and then move to "the next big idea." There's often no expressed coherence between this change and that change. We'll get at why that is so in a moment.

### Recognizing the Power in Others

Listen to part of our interview with **Mike Oliver**, principal of Zaharis Elementary School, Mesa, Arizona, where he talks about realizing the importance of creating an environment where people can take risks and think creatively. (Listen via the QR code at the end of this chapter, or click on Link 1.3 at www.shiftingforimpact.com.)

### Figure 1.2   Macro and Micro Changes in Education

**Macro initiatives—federal and state mandates**

| | |
|---|---|
| • Common Core | • Next Generation Learning Standards |
| • ESSA | • No Child Left Behind |
| • High-stakes assessments | • Standards-based instruction |

**Micro initiatives—thought leader driven**

| | |
|---|---|
| • 1:1 computing | • Mindfulness |
| • Authentic learning | • Personalized learning |
| • Backwards design | • Professional learning committees |
| • Climate and culture committees | • Project-based learning |
| • Coaching for performance | • Reading in the content area |
| • Cooperative learning | • Response to intervention |
| • Critical thinking | • Restorative justice |
| • Differentiated instruction | • Rubric-based appraisals |
| • Flipped learning | • Social and emotional learning |
| • Formative assessments | • Standards-based grading |
| • Game-based learning | • STEM |
| • Growth mindset | • Student-centered learning |
| • Instructional rounds | • Students as creator |
| • Integrated thinking | • Visible learning |

These changes all come from well-intentioned "thought leaders," many of whom labor *outside* of the school buildings and classrooms and, especially with the micro changes, recommend changing a narrow aspect of education defined by their particular interest. Because the impetus for change is coming from the outside, practitioners quickly find themselves in a position of being reactive rather than proactive to change. They are left to adapt and attempt to establish coherence—or not.

Practitioners are often whipsawed by these well-intentioned "supports," which leads skeptics and exhausted staff to view many changes as fads, fashions, initiatives, and, worst of all, panaceas. Michael Fullan and Joanne Quinn (2016) speak to this consequence when they argue against "initiative overload and fragmentation" in their book, *Coherence*.

The teacher educators with whom we spoke echoed this concern. To paraphrase their observations—and they understandably wanted to remain anonymous—"It seems like every year we try a 'new' educational initiative—something that someone read about or experienced at a conference. We never seem to stay with it, though, because there's always something new following on its heels. And our problems remain the same."

It's no wonder that educators become cynical about change and sit with their arms crossed as the latest change initiative is announced. They don't have to say it, but we know what they're thinking: *This too shall pass.* Dr. Mary Howard remarked in our interview, "You can't have a different program every year. You can't buy your way to change. We have to stop playing the initiative game."

### Shift 3: Change How We Look at Change

The first task of leadership at this juncture is to do something totally counterintuitive in today's world of work, be it business or education, and that is to pause. Here's why. As Michael Bunting (2016) describes in his thoughtful book, *The Mindful Leader*,

> Architect, theorist, and inventor Buckminster Fuller once mused that 5000 years ago an invention or innovation that changed what he called "the critical path of humanity" came along about every 200 years. By AD 1 the interval had decreased to 50 years, and by AD 1000, 30 years. By the Renaissance, an invention that changed the nature of our world was emerging every three years; by the Industrial Revolution, it was happening every six months; and by the 1920s, Fuller estimated, the interval was down to 90 days. He called this extraordinary process "accelerating acceleration." Physicist Peter Russell suggests the interval between important new breakthroughs is now down to days, if not hours. (Bunting, 2016, p. 88)

Given this rapid pace of external change, school leaders need to be extraordinarily mindful of how change is currently managed and perceived internally. To do that, they must take stock of their current change culture relative to their organizational why. They must step off the moving sidewalk, the frenetic putting-out-the-fire management of the day to day and . . . pause. Pausing, author Kevin Cashman (2012) notes in *The Pause Principle*, "helps us focus our attention and our energy." And by doing that, leaders begin to ask better questions, listen better, synthesize, and challenge the status quo.

Reactive and transactional changes will be challenged to support the organizational why—if there is one—because staff will tend to see change initiatives as "the flavor of the month" and disconnected with everyone running from one side of the proverbial sinking boat to the other. Conversely, proactive and cohesive change initiatives will first be looked at through the lens of a critical question: "How is this proposed change legitimately related to other change activities we've undertaken or are considering in support of our organizational why?"

## LEADERSHIP SPOTLIGHT

Pause for mindful metacognition: Reflect on what's happening around you; what's working and not working; what you're thinking, feeling, and learning; and how you're managing your emotions and relating to others.

With a shift toward such a culture, change becomes more internally driven and purposeful toward achieving the organizational why. It can still benefit from outside influencers, but it's not solely dependent on them for inspiration.

*The Bottom Line*—Leaders need to shift the impetus for change from outside the district or school to the inside. They do this by creating a culture that constantly looks for ways to sustain progress toward achieving their organizational why through a series of ongoing and coherent activities. And of critical importance, leaders need to create the expectation that all initiatives, decisions, and actions will be measured against their ability to support the desired impact the organization wants to have on behalf of those they serve.

## Try This

1. Which of the principles of the leader–leader model do you consistently demonstrate?

2. Where do you still default to a leader–follower model?

3. Why would some leaders be reluctant to operate within the leader–leader model?

(For more on Captain Marquet's story, watch his illustrated talk *Inno-Versity Presents: "Greatness" by David Marquet*, which is available on YouTube and at Link 1.4 Captain Marquet Video.)

  Scan this QR code or visit the website at
www.shiftingforimpact.com
to access the links listed above.

# Who You Need to Be as a Change Leader 2

Successful change leaders focus as much on the *who* of change—including themselves—as they do on the *what* and *how*.

**THE BIG SHIFT**

## A LEADER'S STORY

Do the Leaders Have What They Need?

Greg Ewing, superintendent
Las Cruces, New Mexico

One of the first things I noticed coming into the district was that the existing structure of central office had all administrators and central office staff reporting directly to the superintendent. You can't have over one hundred executives reporting to you and be effective with them. On top of that, 30 of the 41 principals had less than three years of leadership experience. They were constantly reacting to situations instead of focusing forward and planning for what should be occurring in the future in their schools. To use a sports analogy, instead of playing offense, they were playing defense all day.

So we had a lot of conversations about how to prepare people to be leaders, not just managers. Ultimately, we started training principals and assistant principals. We created courses within an overall leadership academy for existing and aspiring administrators and principals. We've worked very hard at focusing on leadership, and we talked extensively about growing talent—about the difference between micromanaging individuals and giving them knowledge and empowering them to make decisions.

## The Leadership Development Challenge

Greg Ewing's experience is not unique. Some of the relatively new school leaders he experienced might have risen to the position because of their strong past performance in the classroom or as a coach on the athletic field. Other young prospects may have pushed themselves into consideration by management for a leadership role for a variety of reasons—not all of them admirable.

Regardless, new educational leaders often (usually?) find themselves in a position where

- they've received no formal leadership training prior to starting in the role or
- the "leadership" training they have received focused largely on the mechanics or *management* aspects of the position: scheduling, facility maintenance, performance measurement, budgeting, legal compliance, safety, and so on. And then,
- formal leadership training is often arranged when things don't go well.

We know this training pattern is true at for-profit and nonprofit organizations alike because U.S. institutions and individuals spend a shocking $14 billion a year to support leadership development. Such development can come in the form of assessments, books, and other materials; conference attendance; workshops; one-on-one coaching; and so on (Hedges, 2014).

In many cases, the training is not effective for a variety of reasons. It's *not*

- individualized,
- usually done in the context of the work performed,
- measured against desired outcomes, and
- longitudinal—developed over time.

And perhaps most important, the training is *not*

- built to address the root cause of participants' poor leadership, which is usually mindset—how they view the leader's role.

So what type of leadership *is* required to lead a successful complex change initiative? In this chapter, we'll look at

- the two broad categories that define the entire landscape of leadership mindset and behavior—and which one should dominate;

- the seven competencies that high-performing school leaders tend to demonstrate; and

- the single most effective mindset and behavior from which all others spring.

## Smart and Healthy Behaviors

The roots of ineffective leadership development start to become clear when we look at the phenomenon that Patrick Lencioni (2012) outlined in his book, *The Advantage*—the difference between what he calls "smart" and "healthy" behaviors leaders tend to exhibit in organizations.

> Smart organizations are good at those classic fundamentals of business—subjects like strategy, marketing, finance, and technology—which I consider to be decision sciences. But being smart is only half the equation. Yet somehow it occupies almost all the time, energy and attention of most executives. The other half of the equation, the one that is largely neglected, is about being healthy. A good way to recognize health is to look for the signs that indicate an organization has it. These include minimal politics and confusion, high degrees of morale and productivity, and very low turnover among good employees. (Lencioni, 2012, p. 5)

Here's the important implication of Lencioni's research. Organizations and leaders tend to have a symbiotic relationship. The demonstration of smart and healthy behaviors will be a reflection of the organization's cultural underpinnings and its leaders' philosophy of leadership. Ideally, leaders and organizations need to keep their eyes on both sets of factors.

Lencioni's model focused on the business world. In Figure 2.1, we've adapted the thinking for the education environment to provide examples of where *smart* reflects the work to be done and *healthy* focuses on the people doing the work.

## Figure 2.1   Smart and Healthy School Leadership Behaviors

| Smart leaders tend to focus on the work | Healthy leaders tend to focus on the people doing the work |
|---|---|
| **Instruction**—meeting the academic needs of all learners | **Motivating vision**—establishing alignment and commitment around a motivating vision that includes all stakeholders |
| **Scheduling**—ensuring the smooth management of school activities | **Building staff capacity**—using self-selected professional learning and coaching to grow leaders at all levels |
| **Security and safety**—establishing protocols for drills and emergencies, and assessing the condition of the physical plant and operations for the safety of students and staff | **Stressing collaboration**—establishing structures and routines that reduce politics, engender teamwork, minimize roadblocks, and promote clear communication |
| **Behavior management**—creating and implementing policies and protocols that promote student behaviors that support a positive learning environment | **Nurturing growth**—building a culture of curiosity, innovation, and learning that recognizes the need for proactive change and continuous improvement |
| **Student performance data**—collecting and analyzing data to identify trends in student performance that can be used to improve instruction | **Communicating expectations**—driving high levels of stakeholder engagement that result in increased ownership and responsibility toward achieving desired results |
| **Teacher evaluation**—conducting classroom observations and completing written evaluations in compliance with district guidelines | **Leveraging classroom observations**—using them as an opportunity to evaluate instruction and identify teachers' professional learning needs |

Like their business counterparts, most school leaders still tend to focus on the smart factors for two understandable reasons:

- Those factors are concrete.
- Many of the factors focus on keeping the school operating smoothly and safely in compliance with rules and regulations. These are critical areas where education leaders were trained and are required to focus. It's an area where they're comfortable.

Conversely, the healthy-side factors can be seen as, well, touchy-feely. They deal with *people*, emotions, and relationships. They're anything but concrete. As a result, when leaders avoid the healthy factors, it's often because they believe

- paying attention to them detracts from limited time,
- these factors are difficult to quantify,
- they'll lose control, and, perhaps most importantly,
- they don't know how.

The implication of this imbalance relative to what we discussed in Chapter 1 is serious. If successful change is in great part the result of *human* behaviors—a focus on the people leading and executing the change—then an inordinate focus on the smart factors is likely to doom change initiatives from the start.

## Highly Effective Leadership Behaviors

In October 2000, Robert Goffee and Gareth Jones published an article in the *Harvard Business Review* provocatively titled "Why Should Anyone Be Led by You?" In the twenty years since, it has consistently remained among HBR's fifty most popular articles. We think it sits in that select group because it was a watershed of sorts in two ways.

First, instead of another article on strategy, competition, return on investment, or marketing tactics, this article spoke about engaging and inspiring people. It spoke of the need for leaders to demonstrate vulnerability, personal weakness, and "tough" empathy—"give people what they need, not what they want." It spoke of the need to interpret *soft data*—data gleaned through listening to and observing people in action. It spoke of the need to fully utilize one's strengths. And while the article didn't specifically tie these healthy-side behaviors to outcomes, the authors concluded, "Great results may be impossible without them" (Goffee & Jones, 2000, p. 4).

Since the publication of the article, researchers and thought leaders have published thousands of articles on how to improve leadership behaviors. Some of that content was specifically targeted toward school leaders. Of this latter group, perhaps none is more relevant to our focus on the change leader than the work done by educational researcher and consultant Lyle Kirtman.

### Kirtman's Seven Competencies of Highly Effective School Leaders

Over the past thirty years, Lyle Kirtman has assessed, observed, and interviewed more than three thousand school leaders from all over the country with one goal in mind: to identify the behavioral characteristics of those school leaders who consistently perform at the highest level. His research eventually pointed to seven competencies. Figure 2.2 outlines key behaviors within those competencies that high-performing school leaders share.

Clearly, these would be admirable behaviors to demonstrate even if we weren't focusing on school leaders as change agents. But when we look at these behaviors from the perspective of change, they become even more powerful.

## Figure 2.2 Kirtman's Seven Competencies of Highly Effective School Leaders

| Competency | Behavioral Hallmarks |
| --- | --- |
| 1. Challenges the status quo | • Challenges common practices and traditions if they are blocking possible improvements<br>• Looks for innovations to support outcomes<br>• Does not let rules and regulations block efforts to achieve outcomes |
| 2. Builds trust through clear communication and expectations | • Is direct and honest about performance expectations<br>• Follows through with actions on commitments<br>• Makes sure there is a clear understanding based on written and verbal communications |
| 3. Creates a commonly owned plan for success | • Creates measurable short- and long-term written plans with input of stakeholders<br>• Ensures that staff commit to the plan<br>• Monitors implementation and adjusts the plan based on new data and communicates changes clearly |
| 4. Focuses on team over self | • Hires the best people for the team<br>• Commits to the ongoing development of a high-performance leadership team<br>• Empowers staff to make decisions in support of intended outcomes |
| 5. Has a high sense of urgency for change and sustainable outcomes | • Sets a clear direction for the organization<br>• Can be very decisive so as to move change initiatives forward quickly if need be<br>• Builds systemic strategies to ensure sustainability of change |
| 6. Commits to continuous improvement for self | • High sense of curiosity and willingness to find and or develop new ways to achieve desired outcomes<br>• Listens to all team members to change practices to obtain results<br>• Strong self-management and self-reflection skills; takes responsibility for their own actions—no excuses |
| 7. Builds external networks and partnerships | • Understands their role as being a part of a variety of external networks for change and improvement<br>• Strong ability to engage people inside and outside in two-way partnerships<br>• Uses technology to expand and manage a network of resources |

*Source:* Adapted from Kirtman and Fullan (2016). Used with permission.

*Numbers 1 and 5*—"Challenges the status quo" and "Has a high sense of urgency for change and sustainable outcomes"—speak to the theme we introduced in Chapter 1: that change needs to be looked at not as a series of independent events but as a cohesive set of actions working toward desired and sustained outcomes.

Here, the change leader demonstrates proactivity. Leaving things as they are—the status quo—won't ensure that the organization fully supports those it serves. Stay the same and the organization gets stale, maybe even backslides, and desired outcomes remain out of reach. Mike Oliver, principal of Zaharis Elementary School in Mesa, Arizona, explained in our interview that he had to confront the status quo issue head-on when he assumed the principal role: "We were doing the same old thing better than probably everybody else, but it was still that same old thing, and I wasn't interested in doing the same old thing."

With these competencies, the change leader demonstrates and encourages curiosity—asking questions about what will work and why. Commensurate with that, they're not afraid to experiment, to innovate to see what works.

There is a pressing need to move expeditiously because the needs of those the organization serves are critical. But speed for the sake of speed is not the goal. As we'll see in subsequent chapters, pace has to be a function of experimentation, iteration, and learning about what change works.

Finally, the change leader carefully monitors compliance and rule following. Strong compliance in legal and financial matters, for example, is critical. But in other areas—following some directives from the state, for example—minimum compliance may be all that's necessary. Attempting perfection here may drain time and energy from more important tasks.

*Numbers 2, 3, and 4*—"Builds trust through clear communication and expectations," "Creates a commonly owned plan for success," and "Focuses on team over self"—emphasize that change has to be proactive, innovative, and timely. But change activity also has to be measured with respect to those helping to plan and implement it. Suggested changes that lack cohesiveness with other changes, are absent a well-thought-out plan, or don't seem to support desired outcomes or the organizational why will be met by your faculty's crossed arms.

The change leader, then, is a strong believer in the team and its front-line wisdom. Commitment to building and owning the change plan is essential, or things fall apart during implementation. Commitment is usually unattainable if the plan is handed down from on high.

Nurturing that commitment is the leader's clear explanation about why a change is needed—the inspiring and engaging vision behind the direction—and expectations about the team's role.

Evan Robb, part of whose interview we shared in Chapter 1, demonstrated this type of thinking when he discovered that transportation funding was cut from the after-school academic support program that he and his staff considered critical to students' success:

> I had some ideas for how to fix it, but instead, we had a faculty meeting, and I said we need to pull together a group of six to ten staff members to solve this problem. How can we look differently at providing some extra support or enrichment for our kids? I asked for a faculty-driven solution. Over a course of six meetings, staff developed a plan to provide students support.

*Number 6*—"Commits to continuous improvement for self"—acknowledges that the change leader must evolve just as the organization must evolve. This is, perhaps, the most important behavior. As we will see later in this chapter and again in Chapter 4, fully understanding and appreciating oneself is a requirement for understanding and appreciating others. *Indeed, it is one of the foundations of all purposeful and impactful change.* Demonstrating appreciation for personal growth communicates to staff that while you may be the change leader, you don't hold yourself apart from or above the organization.

*Number 7*—"Builds external networks and partnerships"—reflects that change leaders are resourceful leaders. They look beyond the confining walls of the school or the virtual walls of the district for support. They recognize that the immediate community has a vested interest in the strength of students walking across the stage to receive their diplomas.

Demonstrating one or more of the competencies can significantly impact outcomes, but in our interview, Kirtman added a note of caution.

> When leaders consistently and authentically demonstrate these competencies, staff will respond with energy and commitment. The key words here are *consistently* and *authentically*. Staff may initially be slow to respond if they've experienced dissonance in the past between what the leader says and how they act or if such attempts have been short-lived. Leaders, too, may stumble trying to demonstrate these competencies if their underlying authenticity is not in place.

### Goleman's Six Defining Leadership Behaviors

Daniel Goleman (2002) defines *resonance* in his seminal work, *Primal Leadership*, as "leaving people uplifted and inspired even in a difficult moment. When a leader triggers resonance, you can read it in people's eyes. They're engaged and they light up" (Goleman, 2002, p. 20). *Inspired* and *engaged* here sound a lot like what Goffee and Jones noted in "Why Should Anyone Be Led by You?," doesn't it?

Goleman's research showed that successful leaders—in this case, leaders who delivered strong financial returns—*appropriately* demonstrated any one of six leadership behaviors in a given situation, with a corresponding impact on resonance.

1. Visionary—moves people toward shared dreams

2. Coaching—connects what a person wants with the organization's goals

3. Affiliative—creates harmony by connecting people to each other

4. Democratic—values people's input and gets commitment through participation

5. Pacesetting—meets challenging and exciting goals

6. Commanding—soothes fears by giving clear direction in an emergency

We emphasize *appropriately* because, according to Goleman, leaders can easily abuse Numbers 5 and 6 (Goleman, 2002).

What, then, can we in education take away from this set of business world behaviors, especially in how they relate to the educational change agent leader?

- To begin with, school leaders may not be working toward *financial* returns, but they are working toward *returns*— desired outcomes and impact on behalf of those the school or district serves. When used appropriately, these behaviors can inspire and increase staff engagement in working toward desired outcomes.

- Next, we can construct a reasonable alignment between Goleman's and Kirtman's research-revealed leadership behaviors, and our ARC model to create a powerful picture of desired leadership behaviors in the context of change.

### Leadership Behaviors and the ARC Change Model

As we see in Figure 2.3, Kirtman's and Goleman's competencies can easily be categorized under *smart* or *healthy*. While many of these behaviors cross over the two behavioral categories, for simplicity's sake, we are only showing them where we feel they best fit. The clear conclusion is that school leaders who demonstrate these behaviors will be straddling both the smart and healthy categories of the leadership landscapes, which, of course, is the goal.

And of equal importance to our focus on change, these behaviors support the ARC change model we introduced in the preface. That is, change leaders would exhibit one or more of these behaviors in each of the three phases of our change model.

Now, one final very important point: Most of the desired behaviors fall on the healthy side of the illustration. This organization of Kirtman's and Goleman's effective leadership behaviors reinforces one of the major philosophical points underlying our book: *Change success is as much or more dependent on the people leading it and executing it as it is on the change itself.*

### Figure 2.3  The ARC Model of Effective Leadership Behaviors

| Phases of the ARC Change Model | Smart Behaviors | Healthy Behaviors |
|---|---|---|
| *Assess* | Challenges the status quo | Creates a commonly owned plan for success<br><br>Visionary—moves people toward shared dreams |
| *Ready* | Builds external networks and partnerships | Democratic—values people's input and gets commitment through participation<br><br>Builds trust through clear communication and expectations<br><br>Focuses on team over self<br><br>Coaching—connects what a person wants with the organization's goals<br><br>Affiliative—creates harmony by connecting people to each other |
| *Change* | Has a high sense of urgency for change and sustainable outcomes<br><br>Pacesetting—meets challenging and exciting goals | Commanding—soothes fears by giving clear direction in an emergency<br><br>Commits to continuous improvement for self |

**Breaking the Mold of the Conventional High School**

Listen to part of our interview with **Rona Wilensky**, creator and first principal of New Vista, an alternative high school in Boulder, Colorado, and **Ivette Visbal**, a founding faculty member and currently the school's dean of students. Listen for evidence of how these two leaders wanted to change the concept of high school education relative to instruction, student choice, responsibility, and community involvement. Listen, too, for how *healthy* played into their thinking about the school culture. (Listen via the QR code found at the end of this chapter, or click on Link 2.1 at www.shiftingforimpact.com.)

## The Most Important Mindset and Behavior

We mentioned earlier that Goffee and Jones's 2000 article, "Why Should Anyone Be Led by You?," was a watershed of sorts in two ways. The first way was how it spoke to the need for the leader to demonstrate healthy-side behaviors—to demonstrate vulnerability, personal weakness, and "tough" empathy; to listen to and observe staff in action; and to fully utilize one's strengths.

The second watershed was Goffee and Jones's tantalizing use of a word that has since received so much print and airtime that it is now almost thread-worn. It's one of those words that we're instinctively drawn to. We want to stand in its glow and wrap ourselves in its truth—a truth we *think* we understand and *think* we demonstrate but, in actuality, usually don't. Goffee and Jones ended the article by counseling leaders that if they were truly going to inspire and engage, they had to be *authentic*.

### What Is Authenticity?

Bill George (2003), the former CEO of Medtronic, a global leader in medical technology, services, and solutions, is arguably the inspirational wellspring when we think about authenticity. In his groundbreaking work, *Authentic Leadership*, he described the five characteristics of authenticity, which we detail in Figure 2.4.

What we should notice immediately about these characteristics is that they are entirely healthy in nature—but with a twist: they are not entirely about the *other*. A big part of authenticity is, of course, all about *you*—really knowing your passions, motivations, and personal beliefs; wanting to connect with staff, not out of obligation but out of curiosity; wanting to convey to staff through your words *and* actions. Authentic

## Figure 2.4    Characteristics of Authenticity

```
                          ┌──────────────┐
                          │ Authenticity │
                          └──────┬───────┘
     ┌──────────┬───────────┬────┴─────┬──────────────┬──────────┐
┌──────────┐ ┌────────┐ ┌──────────────┐ ┌──────────────┐ ┌──────────┐
│  Self-   │ │ Values │ │ Relationships│ │Self-discipline│ │ Purpose  │
│direction │ │        │ │              │ │              │ │          │
└────┬─────┘ └───┬────┘ └──────┬───────┘ └──────┬───────┘ └────┬─────┘
┌──────────┐ ┌────────────┐ ┌────────────┐ ┌────────────┐ ┌────────────┐
│Understand-│ │Identifying │ │Connecting  │ │Living one's │ │Conveying   │
│ing one-   │ │personal    │ │directly    │ │values      │ │organiza-   │
│self, one's│ │beliefs;    │ │with staff  │ │through     │ │tional      │
│passions,  │ │speaking    │ │on an       │ │one's       │ │purpose to  │
│purpose,   │ │with        │ │emotional   │ │actions     │ │staff       │
│and under- │ │integrity   │ │level       │ │            │ │            │
│lying      │ │            │ │            │ │            │ │            │
│motivations│ │            │ │            │ │            │ │            │
└──────────┘ └────────────┘ └────────────┘ └────────────┘ └────────────┘
```

*Source:* Adapted from George (2003, pp. 36–37).

leadership in that regard is about both the *who* and the *what* of the work. Lead from that dual mentality, George (2003) argues, and the rest will follow. We'll revisit authenticity in Chapter 6, where we discuss the integral role it plays in developing emotional intelligence.

Now, here's the most critical point about authenticity. As author Kimberly Davis (2018) describes in *Brave Leadership*, "In the framework of leadership and influence, the people around you get to decide—your direct reports, your team, the people you lead, your boss, your colleagues . . . . These people are your audience. They get to decide if you're authentic. You do not" (p. 35). In our interview, Principal Evan Robb agreed: "There has to be congruence between what you say and what you do because if they're not congruent, no one's going to believe what you say—they'll only believe what you do." In short, you don't get to stand in the glow of authenticity or wrap yourself in its truth unless those with whom you work say you can.

The implication of that last point has everything to do with achieving or not achieving desired outcomes. Can you as the leader achieve

## LEADER VOICES

### "What Do People Need From Me?"

Listen to part of an interview we conducted with **Kimberly Davis**, author of *Brave Leadership* (2018). Note where she discusses the need to have an external focus versus an internal one—a focus on serving some higher purpose outside of yourself—to achieve the impact you want to have. And note, too, why being vulnerable challenges us to our core. (Listen via the QR code found at the end of this chapter, or click on Link 2.2 at www.shiftingforimpact.com.)

outcomes without being authentic? Yes, but not on a *sustained* basis. Leadership that lacks authenticity will eventually—soon?—lead to the polar opposite of an engaged staff. (Maybe leaders' inauthenticity is a big factor contributing to that 70 percent disengagement factor we reported in Chapter 1?) Disengagement leads to low productivity and a revolving door of employment. Inauthentic leadership is so nefarious, reported *The Mindful Leader* author Michael Bunting (2016) in our interview, that up to "33% of your mental health and 40% of your engagement at work can be explained by your boss's behavior." It's no surprise, then, that research historically shows the number-one reason people leave an organization is because of the behavior of the person to whom they report.

When we step back and look at the characteristics of authenticity, we have to ask, what holds leaders back from being authentic and demonstrating authentic leadership? Part of the answer lies back where we discussed why many leaders shy away from the healthy side to begin with: Dealing with emotions and relationships can be challenging. But here, we're not talking about the emotions of and relationship to others; we're talking about dealing effectively with your own emotions and being comfortable with the relationship you have with yourself. Authenticity starts at home. It's not something than can be taught in a professional development workshop (or a book!). Those environments can expose us to the constructs and benefits of authenticity, but authenticity isn't fed from the outside; it's fed from the *inside*. It has to be realized and released. Standing in the way of that release are the stories we were told about ourselves when we were young and, even more dangerous, the stories we tell ourselves today.

## Why Is Authenticity First?

Okay, so why the heavy focus on *authenticity*? Simply put, *you cannot lead others effectively until you lead yourself effectively*. Kevin Cashman (2012), author of *Leading From the Inside Out*, makes the point,

> As enterprise leaders, our own advancing personal growth directly influences the dynamic capacity for organizational growth. Before we can grow authenticity and purpose in others, we must dedicate ourselves to our own growth of authenticity and purpose. If we do, our development of others will be powerful, and our credibility will be well earned. We must become the leader we wish to see in our organization. (p. 84)

Leaders seeking to lead, support, and develop others need to heed the wisdom of the old saw: *"Physician, heal thyself."* You cannot lead others effectively until you know how to lead yourself effectively.

And for many reasons, doing so won't be easy. It's hard to look in our own mirror. As Bill George (2015) once noted, "The hardest person you will ever have to lead is yourself" (p. 7).

### The Bottom Line

When we honestly develop it, authenticity becomes that large red arrow in the store directory of your mental mall noting, "You are here." Pathways to all the other desirable behavioral skills—like the pathways to stores in the mall—emanate from that point. It is the engine that drives the creation of a motivating vision, a collaborative spirit, the curiosity to see in others what they may not see in themselves, the excitement around innovating and experimenting, and the desire to coach so as to unleash the wisdom already present in others.

How you can help release your authentic leadership is detailed in Chapters 4 and 6. But in our next chapter, we'll look at how smart and healthy play out in high-performing organizations.

## Try This

As a leader, which type of behaviors do you tend to gravitate toward: smart or healthy? We'll talk more about this in Chapter 4, but if you sense you need to focus more of your attention on the healthy side, try experimenting with these behaviors:

- Be curious. Meet with staff, students, and parents. Listen with intentionality to learn and to develop relationships.

- Stay visible and accessible. Keep your office door open. Spend the bulk of time visiting classrooms. Look for ways to collaborate with people and connect ideas.

- Demonstrate transparency and vulnerability with questions such as "I don't know; what do you think?" or "If this happened, how would it affect you?"

- Collaborate with others to establish protocols to handle common "fire extinguisher" issues that can sap your energy and your time.

- Model behaviors that are consistent with a positive culture (e.g., the behaviors you want to see in others).

As you do, check in with yourself. What was the experience like? What did you feel? How did others react to you? This self-reflection is essential. You need to measure the *internal* impact of behaving more on the healthy side. If you only focus on the external expressions of these behaviors, you're likely to slip back to what you've always known.

What other examples of healthy-side behaviors can you suggest?

 Scan this QR code or visit the website at www.shiftingforimpact.com to access the links listed above.

# What Organizational Principles Support a Culture of Productive Change?

# 3

Understanding organizational culture and how to develop and use it to shape high performance in schools is critical for effectively managing change.

**THE BIG SHIFT**

## Culture—A Driver of Desired Outcomes and Impact

In Chapter 2, we looked at the qualities the leader needs to demonstrate to support effective change. Here, we focus on the organization—and specifically on organizational culture—and ask the critical question, "What are the characteristics of a dynamic culture that uses change wisely to support its *why*?" That is, "What cultural factors help an organization work toward securing its desired outcomes and impact on behalf of the population it serves?" By understanding the concept of organizational culture and how to manage it, leaders can begin using their change efforts to shift their school toward a highly adaptive culture of curiosity, experimentation, and learning.

Organizational culture can be defined as a set of values that organization members share regarding the philosophy and functioning of the organization. It can be thought of as the "personality" of the organization, and it informs people "how things are done here" (Certo & Certo, 2019). Once established, this culture exerts an organizing force over the individuals within the system, and this force is often nearly invisible to its members.

### The Iceberg Model of Culture

In the classic iceberg model of culture, 10 percent of an organization's culture is visible above the waterline while 90 percent is below the surface—not as readily visible—anchoring "how we do things here." Figure 3.1 shows how visible, tangible elements, such as posted signs and school policies, can be held in place by invisible, intangible elements, such as tradition and concepts of leadership. Shifting requires a school leader to address the whole system, including not only formal structures and observable behavior but also digging deeper into shared beliefs, norms, and values and even subconscious fundamental views and assumptions about the way things are. As we'll see later, in Chapter 6, leaders must draw on their emotional intelligence to identify and address such deeply held views.

The concept of organizational culture is important for a leader who is driving change because otherwise the mechanics of "success" or "failure" are somewhat mysterious. Let's say you are a new principal in your building, and to support school safety, you decide to create a strict policy forbidding all food in classrooms. No need to intentionally hang a "Welcome!" sign for those little critters, right? However,

**Figure 3.1   The Iceberg Model of Culture Applied to a School**

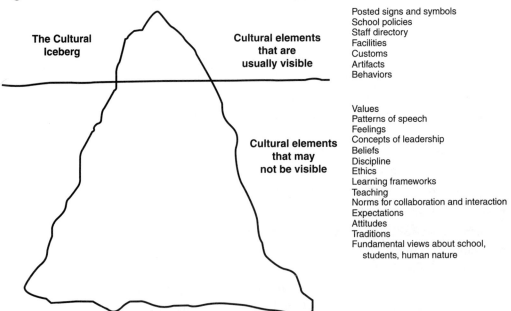

you aren't aware that in the past, there were heated conversations about reducing inequity for students who miss important interactions with peers and adults when they have to eat breakfast in the cafeteria rather than in the classroom. As a result of those conversations, everyone has been bending the rules to accommodate these students.

Your announcement of the new safety policy elicits icy stares and disapproving grumbles. People may not be willing to explain to you, a new principal, why they don't like your new policy, but if you have any emotional intelligence, you can read discontent from their reaction: "That's *not* how we do things here."

To some leaders, seeking to change elements above the waterline is tempting because they're dealing with matters that are highly visible. The school's norms, beliefs, attitudes, and feelings, however, are *below* the waterline, and they very much shape the organizational response. So, if people don't get on board with a change, it's because 90 percent of what drives people is below the waterline. If the change you are seeking requires a significant shift in norms, values, or core assumptions about "who we are and how we do things here," then you should introduce the change with intentionality—devoting the time and energy that the situation warrants to build commitment and achieve the outcome you desire. The following story illustrates the point.

## A LEADER'S STORY

### Introducing a Complex Change With Intentionality

Richard Gonzales, associate professor in residence
Director, Educational Leadership Preparation Programs
University of Connecticut

Dr. Gonzales leads the UConn University Principal Preparation Initiative, a $5.45 million project designed to improve principal preservice training. Historically, individual professors were responsible for a specific class and generally worked independently. Dr. Gonzales observed, "As long as a professor got the syllabus ready and talked with other professors a week or two before class started, they had a lot of instructional freedom. The current semester would proceed, and the professors usually wouldn't see each other until the beginning of the next semester."

*(Continued)*

(Continued)

To strengthen the program on behalf of the population it serves, Dr. Gonzales decided to gradually introduce a major redesign of the program, an element of which was a spiraling instructional delivery approach. Professors would teach multiple courses, reconnect with students over the two-year program, and build on concepts taught by their colleagues. Going forward, professors were asked to work in teams to discuss their shared learning targets and to integrate feedback from colleagues as they assessed a student's progress.

Drawing a parallel to the teacher who allows students to play with manipulatives before structuring how they are to be used in a lesson, he explained that he was "letting the professors get a feel for teaming and what's it's like to teach in a spiraling structure over the course of an entire two-year cycle" rather than handing down specific how-to instructions. Of equal importance, he wanted to give himself time to see how his team reacted to the change. He explained that during this process, "I could see where their natural curiosity and inclinations led them, and I could pay attention to where there was alignment and where there wasn't." In introducing this change, Dr. Gonzales had to consider the faculty's major underlying attitudes and values—in this case, independence and autonomy. If he hadn't, the redesign might have failed.

It's also important to note with respect to Lyle Kirtman's fifth competency for highly effective school leaders (Chapter 2)—*has a high sense of urgency for change and sustainable outcomes*—that Dr. Gonzales in the "Leader's Story" demonstrated an urgency for change relative to the *issue*: He was determined to improve how professors teach their courses and interact with colleagues. However, in recognition of how deep a cultural shift in norms and values this change represented, Gonzales didn't rush the intervention in terms of the *pace*. He proceeded deliberately toward a sustainable, long-term solution that his people would buy into and continue to improve over time.

### Immunity to Change

We'll look more closely at resistance to change in Chapter 6, but it's important to introduce the concept now to underscore the neuroscience behind the need to proceed with intentionality in a complex change. In their book, *How the Way We Talk Can Change the Way We Work*, Robert Kegan and Lisa Laskow Lahey (2001) use the analogy of an immune system to explain how a person (and an organization) can react to a new change. When a change is introduced, it is perceived at some level as a threat, and it activates a system of protection to eliminate the change. This, the authors describe, is the "processes of dynamic equilibrium, which, like an immune system, powerfully and mysteriously tends to keep things pretty much as they are" (p. 5).

Following that metaphor, leaders who are trying to make a successful change must take into account that the organism they want to affect already has an existing culture in place. As the leader, you cannot just give people a new directive, put in place some new policies, and take a few decisive actions to effect change. Instead, you must follow a process of intentional cultivation. You need to recognize the idea that the existing culture is a number of living cells that have formed a symbiotic colony within the organizational petri dish. When you attempt to lead a change, you introduce new elements that may take hold and spread or may be rejected and die without influencing the rest of the organism.

To help prevent rejection, you must guard against looking at a change in isolation. The point we make throughout the book is that changes need to be looked at collectively as nourishing a purposeful culture that increases the likelihood of achieving outcomes and impact.

### Culture—Greater Than the Sum of Its Parts

When leading change, it is necessary to think of the organization as greater than the sum of its individual parts. It is not just made out of the individuals on your staff; not just made of the visible collections of people into departments, teams, and functional areas that show up on an organizational chart; not even just the connective fluids and tissues of inter-team dynamics that surround these areas. It's the entirety of the organizational body itself. The organization you are leading has a life of its own, including a purpose and a history with reasons for being the way that it is, and it has gathered momentum carrying it forward in its current path. A key to unlocking the ability to effect change in the organization as a whole is to look to the organizational culture.

## Smart and Healthy Organizational Cultures

When embarking on a change effort, leaders understandably tend to think of the smart actions to drive the change: getting the goals right, assigning resources, setting up a timeline, and tracking progress. These are all good and necessary actions. However, it's the healthy activities that are most likely to effect long-term changes in the organizational culture because it's people that ultimately open or close the gates of change: honoring traditions and linking those traditions to new efforts, allowing space for different voices, and coaching instead of directing. Such practices intentionally shift "how we do things here," not just to pull off this one change but to become highly adaptive and productive working toward outcomes and impact. Just as we saw in Chapter 2 where leaders need to exhibit both smart and healthy behaviors to be effective change leaders, we're going to argue that effective organizational cultures undertaking a change need to reflect similar smart and healthy thinking.

## Characteristics of High-Performing Cultures

In speaking of the importance of organizational culture, Peter Drucker, a respected authority on leadership, is often credited with the aphorism, "Culture eats strategy for breakfast." If we accept that statement as true, it helps to unpack it: A strong culture will lift up an organization; a dysfunctional one will bring it down. With that truism in mind, we have to recognize that moving from where the organizational culture is now toward a desired future state is not a matter of simple mechanics. We need to get a picture of what a *strong culture* looks like in action.

Researchers who have studied organizational culture have long looked at the relationship between an organization's culture and its ability to consistently achieve short-term *and* long-term goals. Not surprisingly, they have found that culture and performance are often closely tied. In a meta-study of the past decade of research on high-performing organizations, which is defined as an organization that achieves outcomes that are significantly better than those of its peers over an extended period of time, academics Jaewoo Kim and Seung Bang (2013) identified six common characteristics that positively influence the relationship:

1. Empower people and give them freedom to decide and act.

2. Establish clear, strong and meaningful core values.

3. Develop and maintain a performance-driven culture.

4. Create a culture of transparency, openness and trust.

5. Create a shared identity and a sense of community.

6. Develop an adaptive culture to achieve long-term success. (p. 4)

As described in the next section, we see strong evidence of these characteristics in high-performing schools.

## Characteristics of High-Performing Schools

In a widely cited work, G. Sue Shannon and Peter Bylsma (2007) described nine characteristics that high-performing schools demonstrated:

1. Share a clear vision and agreed upon goals.
2. Hold high standards and expectations for all students.
3. Provide effective instructional and administrative leadership.
4. Ensure high levels of collaboration and communication.
5. Align curriculum, instruction and assessment with standards.
6. Improve teaching and learning through frequent monitoring and adjustments.
7. Sustain focused professional development aligned to vision and goals.
8. Create a safe and supportive learning environment.
9. Achieve a high level of parent and community involvement. (p. 1)

The authors make the point that there is no one silver bullet here for sustained performance and that truly successful schools committed to high performance demonstrate a number of these characteristics over many years. Schools throughout the country have used these characteristics as a guide to shape their improvement plans.

The characteristics from both lists are in evidence during a high-performing organization's day-to-day operation, and as we see in Figure 3.2 on the next page, some can be grouped as smart while others are healthy in their focus. This alignment is critical in showing that these behaviors support the three phases of our ARC change model. Not surprisingly, there is strong conceptual alignment between the cultural factors we see in the figure and the leadership factors we introduced in Chapter 2.

How do these characteristics of smart and healthy show up in an actual school? Look for them in the excerpt of our interview with Lamarr Thomas in our "Leader's Story" on page 41. Here, as a newly appointed principal at J. E. Dismus Middle School in Englewood, New Jersey, in 2011, Thomas described what he called the school's "Cultural Renewal Plan."

## Figure 3.2   The ARC Model of Effective Organizational Culture

| Phases of the ARC Change Model | Smart Characteristics | Healthy Characteristics |
|---|---|---|
| *Assess* | • Share a clear vision and agreed-upon goals.<br>• Hold high standards and expectations for all students. | • Establish clear, strong, and meaningful core values.<br>• Create a shared identity and a sense of community. |
| *Ready* | • Provide effective instructional and administrative leadership. | • Empower people and give them freedom to decide and act.<br>• Achieve a high level of parent and community involvement.<br>• Ensure high levels of collaboration and communication.<br>• Create a culture of transparency, openness, and trust. |
| *Change* | • Align curriculum, instruction, and assessment with standards.<br>• Improve teaching and learning through frequent monitoring and adjustments.<br>• Develop and maintain a performance-driven culture. | • Create a safe and supportive learning environment.<br>• Sustain focused professional development aligned to vision and goals.<br>• Develop an adaptive culture to achieve long-term success. |

## Building the Strong Why, Who, and What

Let's now take a deeper dive to see what the characteristics of high-performing school cultures look like behaviorally through the lenses of why, who, and what. We take this approach because the seeds of change failure, as we noted in Chapter 1, are evident in these three categories. If leaders and teams intentionally address these three categories, they increase the likelihood of successful change.

### The Why—Sharing a Clear, Agreed-Upon Purpose

What does a clear *why* look like in an organization? Walk into a school that has one, and you can almost feel the *why* in the air, most likely established through a collaborative effort. While there may be countless needs depending on where one sits in such a school, there is common agreement about the most critical or urgent mission for this school. This shared *why* creates a sense of community, allowing people to see each other as members of one tribe. When visiting Zaharis

## A LEADER'S STORY

"We're going to do this together."

Lamarr Thomas, principal, J.E. Dismus Middle School
Englewood, New Jersey

Our school was sliding at that point—for six straight years we were trending in the wrong direction. I said in order to turn it around correctly, I have to build something that's going to live on beyond me—and to accomplish that, it's going to have to be built organically.

So I decided to spend the first year analyzing things and taking a very hard look at our actual practice. What are our best practices, and what are some of the practices that we've maintained that we need to reconsider? Instead of coming in as the savior, I said, "We are going to do this together." So even before my first day as principal, I met with many community members—many of whom did not have children in the school but had some sort of influence one way or another.

The first year of this plan was all about what was personal to us. How do we think? How do we feel about this? What do you believe about the school that you work in? And it was a year of discovery. We realized that some of the practices that we even protected weren't worthwhile.

So that whole year of discovery really allowed us to have some heart-to-hearts with each other before we opened it up to the broader community. What I promised them in that year of discovery was that we're going to climb into this cocoon one way, but we're going to emerge another way. We want to fly out of it even after crawling into it initially.

The second year of this plan, I concentrated on relationships. How do you relate to one another as peers? Do you share lesson planning? Is there common planning? Are you working in silos? How do our children relate to each other—peer to peer? How do you relate to our children? How does this school relate to the broader community? I had to consider how to build that out—how am I relating as a school to the broader community? Who am I inviting to come in? Who do I want to be in partnership with? I thought this work would take one year, but it was so important, it took two years.

(Continued)

(Continued)

So then, in year three, we moved to purpose. Our purpose is to promote high levels of student achievement. Period. And because of that, I was able to say, "If this is our purpose, now let's revisit what comes with our purpose." Here's where I introduced core values, and we focused on the why. The why is not negotiable. Why we're doing this will never change. The methods can change every year. Strategies, curriculum—all of that can change. Personnel, governance—that can change every year. But the why will never change—the why is the purpose: We will remain culturally relevant and will be relentless in our pursuit for excellence. All of our decisions will be research and data driven. We're trying to ensure that the next generation of problem solvers and critical thinkers will come out of our school.

In the fourth year, I can deal with the structural part: the initiatives, the programs, and who we are formally partnered with.

Last but not least—a very, very important one—is that we're building this beyond the strength of one individual. So this cannot rest completely on the charisma of Mr. Thomas. Yes, I was once a student here. Yes, I'm locally well known. Yes, I have generational relationships and so forth. But this is not my show. We're trying to build a school, not an article for Lamarr Thomas. This is about Dismus Middle School, and so in doing that, we were able to filter what people wanted to do with our core values.

Elementary School in Mesa, Arizona, Mary Howard immediately saw evidence of its intense *why*.

> From the moment I walked into the building, it was different than anything I had ever seen before. We were told that we could go into any classroom. When we went into classrooms, we didn't see sporadic excellence; we saw excellence from one side of the building to the other. Every classroom was built on a spirit of collaboration and dialogue. I knew exactly what that school was about and what the staff stood for when I walked in there.

### The Why Is Visible in the Space

Typically, this agreement is summarized in a simple, repeatable phrase that is front and center in the space—for example, "Creating Tomorrow's Leaders Today," "Achieving Excellence Together," or "A Partnership in Discovery." It can be seen in the physical

### In a Mindful Culture You Can Sense Calm Productivity—Even in a Crisis

**LEADER VOICES**

Listen to part of an interview we conducted with mindfulness expert **Oksana Esberard** where she describes the characteristics a mindful culture would likely exhibit. As she talks, think about the implications of those characteristics on an organization's why and its ability to deliver on behalf of that why. (Listen via the QR code at the end of this chapter, or click on Link 3.1 at www.shiftingforimpact.com.)

environment—on key documents, in conference rooms, within individual teachers' classrooms, and even in the hallways. It is shared with key stakeholders, such as boards of education, state administrators, parents and families, and the broader community of the school.

### The Why Is Known by Everyone

When you talk with people about this clear why—and even the statement itself—they know what it means. They can tell you what it means to the organization, and they can even explain the deeper, personal meaning it has for themselves. Everyone in the school knows what it means, not just administrators or supervisors but all levels of staff and all functional areas, including the support staff.

### The Why Is Translated Into Goals

A healthy school has done the heavy lifting of translating its clear, overarching why into strategic goals that cascade down to each person's individual goals. How each school executes the translation might be different. For example, one might use a well-crafted strategic plan, while another may use yearly or quarterly planning, and still another may translate big-picture goals into specific target metrics that staff aim to achieve.

### The Why Is Actively Used

But to be clear, the why isn't just a flashy marketing statement. Wethersfield's why, which we wrote about in Chapter 2, is a filter that authorizes proposed changes that support it and rejects others that don't. It is ultimately a lens that brings outcomes and impact into focus.

Develop students' use of 21st century skills such as problem solving and critical thinking, nurture their social and emotional character, and increase their civic awareness and behavior so they can successfully navigate in and contribute to an increasingly complex and interdependent world *now*.

You can tell when a school has a clear why because it is used to guide daily actions and key decisions. When considering decisions, people bring up the purpose and ask questions about how the actions they would take will align with and support making this purpose happen. It is referenced during quick touch-base conversations about daily activities. Deep deliberation about this purpose happens during strategic meetings, and it guides these overarching decisions. It is also shared with others to explain why certain decisions were made.

The *now* in Wethersfield's why changes everything. Graduating high school students educated in that environment will walk across the stage to receive their diploma and be better able to use their knowledge and skills in a collaborative way to solve complex problems for the betterment of society.

When there is no shared understanding of the why—the higher purpose of your collective effort—everyone could be off "doing their own thing." Each change effort could be viewed as just another meaningless task, easily becoming a flash in the pan. Intentionally encouraging the development of a cohesive organizational culture guided by a shared why sustains high performance and productive change.

## The Who—Cultivating Leadership Behaviors in Everyone

In a high-performing school culture, everyone is expected to exhibit leadership behaviors—not in the traditional sense of command and control but in how they approach their work—how they think and justify their proposed actions.

At the level of the individual, each person has a strong sense of ownership for their own responsibilities and takes control of their actions as a leader in their own sphere. (We saw this concept in Chapter 2, and we will explore it in greater detail in Chapter 6, where we look at the critical alignment of responsibility, authority, and accountability.) Autonomy—empowering people and giving them freedom to decide and act relative to the agreed-upon why—is embedded in people's assumptions of "how we do things here"; it's part of the culture.

At the level of the organization, there are systems and processes in place that encourage effective collaboration—from simple shared documents providing access to meeting notes to regular town halls designed to gather information and generate ideas. People's diverse perspectives, talents, and insights are intentionally harnessed to inform and drive decisions. Smart and healthy organizations balance being decisive and inclusive. What are examples of how this looks in a school?

### People Know Each Other

In a high-functioning school, people know each other and understand how they are related to each other within the organizational structure. As strange as it may seem, one of the major obstacles to organizational effectiveness is not knowing who is on your team and not knowing what their function is in the system. Simply distributing a printed staff directory (in addition to the online version) with each person's name, function, and a skill for which they are known and placing it in each meeting room and common area could go a long way toward granting more access to the who of your organization.

*A School Example*—In one high-performing school we visited, we noticed one of the bulletin boards in front of the principal's office had been devoted to showcasing the school's support team. The team had a catchy name, everyone's faces were represented with their names below, and it showed their job function. When we asked about it, the administrative assistant who created it said that she originally made the display just as a fun activity before school started but that she had been really surprised by the significant effect it had. The support staff reported feeling more like a valued part of the school, and the teachers and other staff said the display helped them think of who to go to when they needed support.

Knowing who the players are makes it possible for everyone to have access to each other and figure out how to include each other when taking action and making decisions. As we saw in Chapter 2, building meaningful relationships is an aspect of authenticity that effective leaders demonstrate. Truly knowing others in your organization and actively using that understanding in your interactions, especially leveraging them in the work you are doing toward your organizational why, is a major factor in a high-performing organizational culture.

### Collaboration Is Expected and Supported

Instead of working as individuals or in silos within one department or functional area, in a high-functioning school or district, people willingly collaborate. They might do so in short-term engagements, such as setting up training for a technology tool, or in ongoing efforts, such as grade-level or cross-discipline lesson planning. This collaboration is of high quality and is supported through direct guidance that creates shared expectations of "how we work together here."

Direct guidance could include formal staff training that explicitly communicates expectations for collaboration, including guidelines for how to lead and participate in meetings, examples of how to communicate effectively via phone and e-mail, and suggestions on how to resolve conflicts and solve problems. Direct guidance could also include new staff receiving onboarding training that includes cultural expectations. Perhaps the new staff member is assigned a culture mentor who helps them get familiar with "how we try to work together here." We might also expect to see posted signs in meeting rooms that speak to agreed-upon norms, such as the following:

## Our Collaboration Guidelines

✓ Choose to be present and participate fully.

✓ Treat everyone with respect.

✓ Share the airtime.

✓ Be open to new ideas.

✓ Silence or put away technology.

✓ Bring your humor, and have fun!

Direct guidance might also include one-to-one coaching for new staff, people who have moved into new roles, and managers who must support and enhance collaboration.

In such highly collaborative environments, staff have internalized the ground rules for positive interactions, and such rules are in evidence in one-on-one exchanges and in group settings. Toxic behavior is reduced up front through these shared norms, but when necessary, leaders have to step in and address specific behavior that is not in alignment with these expectations. In some extreme cases, individuals who continuously violate the collaboration norms may have to be terminated.

*Why High-Performing Teams Are High Performing*—Researchers have long known that high-performing teams positively impact organizational performance. But only within the last few years did researchers at Google begin to bring greater clarity to the underlying and more important question: What makes these teams high performing in the first place? After an exhaustive three-year study, they concluded that psychological safety was a critical component. *Psychological safety* is a concept that psychologists define as a shared belief held by members of the team that the team environment is safe for interpersonal risk-taking. Team members operating under its umbrella exhibit a high degree of trust in fellow members and feel comfortable being themselves within that environment.

In Google's case, two characteristics of psychological safety working *simultaneously* were seen to have significant impact on performance: conversational turn-taking and empathy. Conversational turn-taking, as its name implies, means everyone gets a chance to speak. Empathy speaks to the idea that instead of listening to respond, team members engage in active listening so as to better understand the emotions underlying what's being said. In short, emotions were not only permitted, they were validated. Sensitivity to others was not only desired, it was expected. Respect for others was paramount (Duhigg, 2016).

*High-Performing Teams Are Empowered*—Team members are encouraged to work together to identify issues and agree upon solutions to implement. They are expected to take ownership of their projects and stay in communication with leaders to coordinate major decisions that have school-wide implications. The process for hiring new teachers at Webb School in Navasota, Texas, exemplifies a high degree of staff empowerment. In our interview, Principal Todd Nesloney cited a powerful example.

> I don't sit in on 75 percent of new-teacher interviews. I now have a committee of teachers and instructional aides who volunteer to interview applicants. Then they meet with me and

## LEADERSHIP SPOTLIGHT

Successful teams run on a high-octane mixture of emotional intelligence and empathy. During team formation, be deliberate in getting agreement on norms that recognize team members as emotional beings first, with the need to demonstrate listening for understanding and conversational turn-taking.

explain why the person would be a good fit and how they'd fit into our culture—or why they wouldn't be a good fit. Successful applicants are asked to teach a demonstration lesson. Again, I don't sit in and watch the lesson. I have the teacher in that class assess the lesson because it's their class, the students are theirs, and they're the experts in that room.

Facilitating the formation of such a team and encouraging its development is a key leadership activity. Such teams give each person who participates a forum in which they are practicing and improving their own leadership skills.

### Intentional Inclusion Is Built Into Key Decisions

Another way to cultivate leadership in everyone is in determining how decisions are made. In a high-performing school, there is careful consideration given to when and how to include staff in decision making. Thoughtful leaders avoid the two extremes—neither restricting important decisions to just their trusted direct reports nor inviting literally everyone to weigh in indiscriminately. Instead, they manage to balance between being decisive and inclusive. They consider what level of participation best fits each situation: Do they want to inform, consult, involve, collaborate, or empower staff? Recognizing that, they design their approach to inclusion to fit their intention. Figure 3.3 illustrates how decision-making roles for both the leader and select staff will change depending on the role they are charged with playing in a given situation.

This idea of intentional inclusion is important to note here because it underscores one of Goleman's six leadership behaviors we discussed in Chapter 2—democratic—which he defines as valuing people's input and getting commitment through participation. When critical decisions affecting more than one person's area of responsibility are identified, thoughtful leaders seek input and ask key people on the ground who are most aware of the details to suggest options. When appropriate, consensus in decision making is sought, understanding that real buy-in and commitment to decisions can result from being included in this process. The definition of consensus we are using here does not mean general or even total agreement. Instead, it means the participants have had the opportunity to share their insights and feel they've been heard, and the resulting decision is one to which they contributed and are now willingly committing to carrying out.

Designing intentional inclusion is especially important when solving complex problems. Leaders may even involve staff in analyzing

## Figure 3.3 The Ladder of Participation in Decision Making

| Leader's Goal for Staff | Level of Staff Participation |
|---|---|
| Empower | Your Intent: Your staff will take full responsibility and ownership for planning and implementing this activity. They will make all decisions.<br><br>Their Experience: "I can take charge of this now." |
| Collaborate | Your Intent: Your staff should be actively partnering with you (and others if needed) to plan, make decisions, and implement this project.<br><br>Their Experience: "I am part of the team working together to get this done." |
| Involve | Your Intent: You need staff to come up with ideas to be considered. You will make final decisions. You also want their contribution to implementation.<br><br>Their Experience: "I am needed for my ideas and assistance on this project." |
| Consult | Your Intent: You want to gather information, consider multiple perspectives, and get advice before you make decisions.<br><br>Their Experience: "My experience and insights are wanted to help guide our work on this project." |
| Inform | Your Intent: You already have made a decision or have important news to share and you want to communicate this to your staff.<br><br>Their Experience: "I'm being kept in the loop on this issue." |

potential solutions to determine the best course of action in alignment with the organizational why. Once the leader or responsible staff have finalized their decision, they communicate their decision to the rest of the staff. (Link 3.2 at www.shiftingforimpact .com provides a real-world example of this type of decision-making process—one where mission success or failure hung in the balance based on the decision.)

Donna Schilke led a number of successful change initiatives at Smith Middle School in Glastonbury, Connecticut, where she served as principal for ten years. In our interview, she explained, "Sometimes leaders already have the solution to a problem in mind. It's very important not to go into a change thinking that solution is the only one. I've learned that sometimes the ideas that come from sharing and asking others for their opinions and feedback changes everything I wanted to do, and it's better."

In addition to being deliberate about including people, there is a conscious effort to avoid groupthink and instead foster diversity of thinking during planning and decision making. Diversity in this context means deliberately inviting differences of thought, and to value it means that you are listening actively for multiple perspectives, dissenting opinions, marginalized voices, and alternative viewpoints.

Donna Schilke made clear that she values hearing from different perspectives when she remarked during our interview,

> You build your team with people around you that you do have that trust with. But you want some level of conflict in that you don't want everyone to agree with you because change isn't good if it's just something that you roll over everybody. So I think it's important to know that conflict can be used to create good conversation and motivation. Challenge to change is good—don't be afraid of it.

Part of respecting differences is acknowledging power differentials (i.e., certain voices are more likely than others to get airtime or influence others given social dynamics). Therefore, actively adjusting interactions to boost marginal voices is key to ensuring diversity of thought. For example, if there is an important decision-making meeting about a discipline policy, making sure to get input from a custodian might unlock a key aspect of the after-school situation that would lead to a breakthrough. Depending on the complexity of the topic, use of an external trained facilitator or an internal staff member who has strong facilitation skills can ensure that there is a safe, equitable, effective, and efficient forum in which diverse input is gathered and processed. By collecting a multiplicity of data points, it is possible to develop a rich, complex picture of what is happening and generate more options for addressing issues.

One critical expectation that underlies an inclusion culture is that everyone steps up and contributes. Inclusion is developed by encouraging everyone's active participation in meetings and in regular one-on-one interactions. Instead of playing the role of passive bystanders, faculty and staff are encouraged to be active participants and to

## MAKING SENSE OF IT

Words matter, and these three have specific meanings.

*Diversity:* Includes all the ways people differ and it encompasses all the different characteristics that make one individual or group different from another ("Racial Equity Tools Glossary," 2013).

*Inclusion:* Authentically engaging traditionally excluded individuals and groups into processes, activities, and decision and policy making in a way that shares power ("Racial Equity Tools Glossary," 2013).

*Equity:* The fair treatment, access, opportunity, and advancement for all people while at the same time striving to identify and eliminate barriers that have prevented the full participation of some groups (Kapila, Hines, & Searby, 2016).

see themselves as leaders within their respective areas. (See the leader–leader discussion in Chapter 1.) Faculty and staff members are trained and relied upon to help figure out how to execute their jobs in ways that fulfill the shared why. In doing so, they help inform the scope, timing, and assignment of new work, making it possible for them to later be held accountable with transparency and respect. (For more on the relationship among authority, responsibility, and accountability, see "The Essential Agreement" in Chapter 6.)

In an organization in which people are not on board and empowered, even well-planned change efforts can fail. Cultivating inclusion and effective collaboration principles within your school culture promotes high performance and sustained progress toward greater impact.

## The What—Acting and Then Reflecting to Drive Impact

The third category of behaviors in the high-performing school culture focuses on accountability and learning. These behaviors allow the organization to act and reflect, so as to make maximum progress toward its organizational why. How might this be visible in a school setting?

### Commitments Are Made to Take Specific Actions

The most important factor in creating a culture of accountability is to make it as clear as possible which well-reasoned actions need to be taken. To do so, the leader and team, as we saw previously, would already have translated their organizational why into goals. Next, they would do the work of converting those goals into concrete actions that they're willing to commit to take within a given timeframe. They would ensure that all functional areas agree to these actions. Once they have that assurance, they would communicate the actions to everyone on the staff. Because of that commitment and schedule, there is an increased likelihood that staff would feel more confident that these actions have been agreed upon and will be supported even if the actions will be challenging to accomplish. As a result, people have really internalized what these actions mean in the context of their day-to-day work.

### Course Corrections Are Anticipated

Goals are revisited often over the course of doing work, and there is an expectation that strategies and actions should be adjusted in response to an analysis of current results. When there is a gap between expected and actual results, staff and leaders explore the reasons for

**LEADER VOICES**

**How Do We Need to Behave to Be Successful?**

Listen to part of our interview with **Margaret Zacchei** as she describes the work she led to change the culture and climate of her school by focusing on shared leadership and increasing student and staff engagement. Note how eliciting and using feedback effectively was key to this change effort. (Listen via the QR code at the end of this chapter, or click on Link 3.3 at www.shiftingforimpact.com.)

this gap and address key issues. These "gap-bridging" work sessions are done in a positive, learning-oriented way that takes into account the whole complex system with all of its moving parts so that people feel respected, acknowledged, and even uplifted. When results meet or exceed expectations, a high-functioning team investigates, so those results can be replicated, reinforced, and built upon.

### Ceremonies Acknowledge Accomplishments

When course corrections are viewed as natural and even appreciated, you begin to see such activities not as an end but as a step on a journey. A healthy organization carves out many opportunities to refresh, reenergize, and celebrate its accomplishments. There are formal ceremonies conducted when the team has completed a certain action, when they've met target metrics, and when they've achieved articulated goals.

In addition to these big celebrations, the leadership team pays attention to staff energy levels and builds in intentional energizers as aspects of "how we do things here." Those energizers could be as simple as watching an inspiring video clip together or participating in larger events, such as community service projects, cookie swaps, group walks, potluck luncheons to celebrate a group or event (e.g., administrative assistant day), or school beautification efforts.

Also, these high-performing schools take time to recommit to the big-picture why and the top-level goals. These fun, inclusive activities give everyone a fresh hit of electricity for their internal batteries and help to restore their sense of a community in action. These celebrations are a visible manifestation of your organizational culture, and they are an effective way to engage and activate the invisible beliefs, values, and views that determine your success as a whole.

Without the habit of acting and reflecting as part of "how we do things here," each change effort is more likely to fail, and even more importantly, an organization cannot learn and evolve toward greater impact. Nurturing this cultural habit enables productive change.

## Becoming a High-Performance Culture Cultivator

Reflective leaders will often see a gap between where their organization's culture is now and where it needs to be with respect to desired outcomes and impact. It is likely that they are undertaking many of the actions we have described in a healthy culture—but not everything. They may see that their organization emphasizes accountability but not respect, or inclusivity in decision making but not decisiveness. Of course, we know that culture is always a work in progress since people are coming and going, and environments and even societal attitudes, norms, and worldviews are ever changing in this era of accelerated acceleration.

### The Bottom Line

Leaders don't need to worry that they have to get the organizational culture right before doing anything else. In fact, we believe that an effective leader can use a specific change effort as leverage to help make cultural shifts. The more intentional a leader is about this dual purpose, the more effective they are at making the change and the shift at the same time. In the chapters that come, we will show how using our ARC model of change will help a leader and the organization get smarter and healthier in "how we do things here." They will use the power of change to shift into a highly adaptive culture of curiosity, experimentation, and learning to support the population they serve.

## Try This

Review the ARC model for effective organizational culture seen in Figure 3.2 on page 40, and then consider the questions that follow.

1. Which of the characteristics is most natural for you to cultivate as a leader? Which seem most natural in your current organizational culture?

2. Which characteristic do you tend to emphasize under stress? Which gets minimized?

3. Which of these characteristics seem most in opposition? Which pair seems more like two sides of the same coin?

Scan this QR code or visit the website at
www.shiftingforimpact.com
to access the links listed above.

# Assessing Your Leadership 4

Increasing one's self-awareness helps you look through a wide lens to better know and manage yourself, know and interact effectively with others, and evaluate the organization's progress toward meeting its why.

**THE BIG SHIFT**

## A LEADER'S STORY

Pause and Listen to Yourself

Mike Oliver, principal, Zaharis Elementary School
Mesa, Arizona

"You know, Mike," said my new principal after I had walked her through our building—I was assistant principal at the time—"there is a different theoretical stance for learning than what I'm seeing here."

And I said, "Really!? What is it?"

"Well, from what I saw, there sure were a lot of kids sitting in rows of desks staring at the backs of other kids' heads with a no. 2 pencil and a worksheet in their hand," she observed.

I looked at her like "Duh! It is a school! What did you expect that you were gonna see?" I couldn't even envision any other possibility. And that was when she gave me a book—and I'm actually looking at my books right now. You can see that there are books all the way around my office—and the book was titled *A Case for Constructivist Classrooms*. I read this

*(Continued)*

(Continued)

book, and it gave me a completely different theoretical orientation for what it means to be a learner.

That story and others make me wish I could go back to the younger version of Mike Oliver so I could say to him, "Son, I'm your future self—not only do you not know everything like you think you do, but there will be other hills that you need to climb, and for that, you're going to need a more open mind than you're demonstrating right now."

## The Importance of Pausing to Reflect

Here, we witness one of the most powerful personal skills you can demonstrate: pausing to self-reflect. As introduced in Chapter 1, pausing to self-reflect yields powerful benefits. It gives us the necessary space to tap into "our true nature, our core, our source, our inner Self" (Cashman, 1998, p. 131). Doing so helps you know and walk your values. And it allows you to better see and truly know others and manage your interactions with them. All of this yields a healthier work environment and improved performance on your part and that of the group toward your why.

We're going to put a toe in the water of self-reflection right now. In this chapter, we move into the **assess** phase of the ARC model of change we outlined in the book's preface. Assessing allows you to take stock of your situation—including yourself, your organization, and your environment—so you can better understand the full picture and then clearly define what impact you intend to have and what problem you are trying to solve with a specific change.

We'll help you assess yourself as the leader through a three-step process:

*What?*—To start you off in the direction of self-awareness, we will offer an assessment of our own making where we've purposefully tied the statements to key points covered in Chapters 1 and 2.

*So what?*—After you take the assessment that follows, we'll look briefly at what your scores mean.

*Now what?*—Finally, depending on how you scored, we'll offer some self-coaching questions and activities to encourage growth.

## What? The Self-Assessment

Two notes of caution before you take the assessment:

- The assessment that follows is short. It's not meant to be inclusive of every point around leadership or change leadership specifically. The results are only meant to give you a flavor of your relationship to change, your style as a change leader, how you attempt to understand and work effectively with others, and, finally, how well you know yourself. You could choose to probe deeper by looking into one or more of the commercially available assessments. (See Link 4.1 for a list of these assessments at www.shiftingforimpact.com.)

- All self-assessments—even the commercially available ones—can yield unreliable results. We're human. When we take tests like this, we can consciously or unconsciously try to present a better picture of ourselves. But here's the thing: Unreliable data, at this point, doesn't help you. So look around: No one is watching you, and no one but you needs to see the results.

## Leadership Self-Assessment

Assign a number that reflects how often you demonstrate the behavior reflected in each statement where 1 = *rarely*; 2 = *occasionally*; 3 = *often*; and 4 = *consistently*.

### Part I

____ I suggest changes that will help us achieve our desired outcomes and impact rather than wait for outside sources to dictate action. (proactive vs. reactive; urgency for change)

____ I make sure we define the desired outcome for any specific change and relate it back to the overall impact we're trying to have as an organization. (cultural vs. one time)

____ Once a change has been defined and agreed to, I put most of my energy into supporting those who have to implement or lead the change, including myself. (support the who)

____ I champion what's working in our organization as part of the explanation for why we need additional changes. (support what's already working)

____ I work with as diverse a group of thinkers as possible to develop the change plan. (create a commonly owned plan)

### Part II

____ I manage change as an opportunity to grow thinkers in the organization as opposed to reinforcing a follower mentality. (leader–leader, capacity building)

____ I've started many a discussion with my team by explaining that I don't have all the answers. (transparency, vulnerability)

*(Continued)*

(Continued)

____ I routinely meet with stakeholders—teachers, students, union representatives, parents, board members, community leaders—to understand what's going on. (intentional listening)

____ I communicate the rationale of a change, solicit feedback, adjust the message if necessary, and communicate again. (builds trust through clear communication)

____ I see community members, businesses, and local government as legitimate problem-solving resources I can tap into for support. (external partnerships)

## Part III

____ When evaluating staff performance, I focus most of my attention on helping them make the most of their strengths. (strengths vs. deficit model)

____ I seek out and include those I know to have a different opinion than mine. (diversity)

____ When confronted with a new challenge or staff concern, I pause for a moment to collect my thoughts before responding. (pausing)

____ I can have and share a deep concern for others but not let my feelings impact the decisions I have to make in the best interest of the organization. (empathy)

____ To support a staff member's problem solving, I ask a lot of questions that are designed to help them determine the best course of action for them and the organization. (coaching)

## Part IV

____ I know my deepest held values and demonstrate them at work. (self-discipline)

____ I see setbacks during a complex change as an opportunity to make midcourse corrections that will ultimately help us achieve our desired outcomes and impact. (optimist vs. pessimist)

____ The classrooms and the hallways are my "office." I seek out opportunities to interact with others. (relationships)

____ I recognize that critical nagging voice inside my head, but I've learned to control it. (inner critic)

____ I seek feedback on my leadership style and behavior and look for opportunities to grow. (continuous improvement for self)

## Total the number of points you gave yourself for each section.

|  |  | Tally of Points |
|---|---|---|
| Part I | Relationship to change | |
| Part II | Leadership style | |
| Part III | Understanding and working effectively with others | |
| Part IV | Understanding yourself | |
| | **TOTAL POINTS:** | |

## So What? Guide to Part Scores

18–20: Rockin' it! You can stop reading the book. (Just kidding.)

13–17: Not bad. There are some areas where you can grow, but overall, you get this.

8–12: Let's roll up our sleeves here! We've got some work to do.

5–7: Hmmm.

## A LEADER'S STORY

"That's not me!"

As told by one of the authors who participated in the conversation.

Sarah studied her scores from the self-assessment and put one hand to her lips. Periodically, she would shake her head.

I had just handed out and reviewed the commercial self-assessment results to a group of school administrators. As the other administrators silently reviewed their results or spoke quietly in pairs, I sat down next to Sarah, a vice principal of a high school.

"What do you think?" I asked.

"They're not me," she whispered. She paused and then stated more forcefully, "These results, they're not me."

(Continued)

**(Continued)**

"Which results specifically?" I asked, turning the results so that I could see them.

"All of them!" she expressed through gritted teeth. "I feel like I do demonstrate leadership skills. I do take initiative. I do innovate. I . . ."

Knowing from experience that it doesn't help to repeat that the assessment under question is a valid and reliable instrument, I merely nodded my head to acknowledge her and kept silent so she would continue to hold the floor.

"I had a bad day when I took this. That can affect the results, right?"

I looked directly at her. "Not to a significant degree."

"I want to take it again!" she announced.

"Absolutely," I replied. "We can definitely do that in, say, six months, after we've done some work together."

Sarah squinted at me but said nothing.

"Let's say for argument's sake that these results do reflect your profile at this point in time," I offered. "What's one area you could work on that would have the most impact on your current assignments?"

She sighed and roughly turned the paper back toward her so she could study the results.

"There," she pointed with resignation at one of the data points. "But it's not me."

## Now What? What Do You Need to Work On?

### The Neuroscience of Change: How We Get in Our Own Way

"You know what? It *was* me," Sarah offered after a few weeks of coaching. And she's not alone. Many individuals to whom we've administered assessments over the years have recoiled at one or more of the findings. (We did, too.) What's at work here are psychological forces that can certainly impact individual performance but also negatively impact a change initiative.

## Suppression

A psychologist might suggest that Sarah's reaction is a type of suppression—the conscious process of dismissing unwanted, anxiety-provoking thoughts, recollections, emotions, and desires. Suppression is one way our minds provide a defense mechanism to what we could otherwise perceive as imperfections in our being or performance.

## Cognitive Distortions

We've spoken before about how the brain dislikes ambiguity and wants to make sense of incoming data. This process can become problematic when we knowingly or unknowingly take on and reinforce biased perspectives about ourselves and the world around us over time.

Psychologists refer to these faulty patterns of thinking as cognitive distortions. Some of the more common cognitive distortions are these:

- All or nothing thinking—The world is either good or bad, black or white. Gray doesn't exist.

- Overgeneralization—It happened once; therefore, it must be a constant.

- Jumping to conclusions—We assume we know what another person is thinking or why they behave the way they do.

- Catastrophizing—Going to a very dark and deep place when something bad has happened or when one has made a mistake.

- "Should"—Things we think we ought to do or the way we think we must behave in a certain situation. Not living up to these standards usually results in massive guilt.

### Distortions in Thought

LEADER VOICES

Here we speak with **Courtney Ackerman**, a researcher and writer who focuses on organizational psychology, especially with how it pertains to the areas of well-being and health care. Here she speaks about cognitive distortions, or faulty patterns of thinking. As you listen to her description of a few of these distortions, consider the impact that someone who operates under one or more of these faulty patterns of thinking might have on a complex organizational change. (Listen via the QR code at the end of this chapter, or click on Link 4.2 at www.shiftingforimpact.com.)

### The Inner Critic

Perhaps most insidious is the concept known as the inner critic, the gremlin, the shadow, or the saboteur. In his 2013 TED Talk, "Know Your Inner Saboteurs," Stanford researcher Shirzad Chamine broke down the inner critic phenomenon into a number of specific voices depending on the individual and circumstance: the judge, the controller, the stickler, the avoider, the hyperachiever, the pleaser, the victim, the restless, the hypervigilant, and the hyperrational. (See Link 4.3 at www.shiftingforimpact.com.)

These voices emerge and are nourished during our upbringing and life experiences, and as neuroscience research has shown, they lodge themselves in our brain for life's long haul. Fundamentally, they present themselves as a defense mechanism—trying to protect us from what they see as the certain dangers of change and the crushing feelings of inferiority compared with others.

Unchecked, these voices can leave us almost paralyzed, ill-equipped for productive relationships, and living a life out of alignment with our natural values. Ultimately, we can go through life not fully realizing who we really are and not demonstrating self-compassion that we are still valued even as an imperfect human being.

**LEADER VOICES**

**How You Tell the Story Creates Who You Are**

Here we speak with **Sarah Elkins**, author of *Your Stories Don't Define You, How You Tell Them Will* and a communications coach who specializes in working with clients on the stories they tell themselves—and on what happens to them as a result. (Listen via the QR code at the end of this chapter, or click on Link 4.4 at www.shiftingforimpact.com.)

Relative to our work here, the critical point to remember is that *we do not leave our inner critic at home; we carry its voice into all our daily interactions, including work*. Here are just ten ways the inner critic can raise its head at work relative to change:

1. "Change makes me uncomfortable."
2. "That won't work here."
3. "We tried that once."
4. "We've always done it this way."
5. "If it isn't broke, don't fix it."

6. "Yeah, but . . ."

7. "Leadership would never approve of that."

8. "Being on a team just complicates getting my work done."

9. "I'm just going to keep my mouth shut because people will think my ideas are stupid!"

10. "This document has to be perfect, or you know who will take the blame."

## LEADERSHIP SPOTLIGHT

As a leader, you don't leave your inner critic and bad habits at home. The stories you tell yourself—and *how* you tell them—are a lens into how you get in your own way.

We review these self-defense mechanism concepts in this chapter because we're no longer talking about leadership in general; we're talking about *your* leadership and its impact on the change process and those working in it. And knowing what goes on in that muscle between our shoulders relative to changing is critical if we and others are going to move forward productively.

### Taking Positive Steps

- Look back at your scores for a moment. In which of the parts do you have a deficit or a full-blown crisis? Where do you have strengths, and how might you take advantage of them? If necessary, refocus on the concepts we introduced in Chapters 1 and 2.

- Next, write out responses to the coaching questions within the selected part.

- Finally, try out one or more of the activities listed within the selected part.

### Part I: Relationship to Change: Self-Coaching Questions

1. Which leadership focus do you tend to have: smart—on the work? Or healthy—on the people doing the work? A bit of both? If you tend to have more of a focus on the smart side, what keeps you there? "It's what I know"? "It's where I was

trained to focus"? "We have limited time to do what we need to do"? What are some simple steps you could take to focus more on the people doing the work?

2. What is the composition of your typical change team? Homogeneous—folks who tend to support the change—or heterogeneous—a mixture of those who support it and those who might challenge it? If you tend to knowingly or unknowingly avoid detractors, what's driving that? How do you tend to react with those individuals who challenge you or your assumptions?

### Part I: Relationship to Change: Activities

1. What's going well in your building or in your district? Where is staff firing on all cylinders? What do you have to be proud of as a group? How can you relate those positives to any changes you're contemplating?

2. Make a list of the changes currently underway in your building or district. How many have commonly accepted coherence with your organizational why? Which are the outliers, and how might you bring them into greater coherence with the overall change effort? Relatedly, which of the changes you identified were undertaken proactively versus reactively? What do your responses here indicate about your change philosophy?

### Part II: Leadership Style: Self-Coaching Questions

1. Is your leadership style more leader–leader or "command and control"? If it's the former, what resonates with you about that style? If you tend to gravitate toward the latter, what's comfortable for you there? Knowing that staff tend to be more engaged with the former, if you're in the habit of quickly responding, take a step back and pause. What types of questions are they bringing to you? How is your quick response conditioning them to come to you seeking answers? What kinds of questions can you ask to turn responsibility back on them and help them become thinkers and problem solvers?

2. Revisit "Figure 2.4: Characteristics of Authenticity" in Chapter 2 on page 28. How do your current behaviors stack

up against the five characteristics? If you're not fully exercising one or more of those behaviors, what do you feel is holding you back? It's important here to focus on internal versus external constraints.

**Part II: Leadership Style: Activities**

1. A key aspect of the leader–leader model that we first saw in Chapter 1 is helping staff become expressive thinkers—people who openly share ideas and solutions and don't need to come to you for every decision. This leadership practice helps you in a variety of ways, but it's also energizing for staff. They become leaders in their own sphere rather than just followers. But here's the key: Thinking through problems and coming up with innovative ideas is born of curiosity. How might you begin to approach your staff to unleash their curiosity and problem solving around unresolved issues?

   - Perhaps train them to respond with Captain Marquet's mantra of "I intend to do _____ because_____." (See Chapter 1.)

   - If they come to you with questions you feel they can answer, develop their thinking by pausing before you immediately respond. Perhaps ask them open-ended questions that get them to take responsibility for thinking through the solution. (Much more on this in Chapter 8.)

   - And very importantly, what do you notice about the staff's reaction as you practice this leadership behavior?

2. Note where you sit in meetings. Are you always at the head of the conference table? If you tend to sit there, dislodge yourself, and sit amid everyone else. Note when you speak. Are you usually first, or do you wait to hear from others? If your answer to that last question is "first," sit back and listen to be informed, not just to respond. You may have to ask others to speak first if they're conditioned to hear you speak. What's it like to gather the opinions of others and then speak?

**Part III: Understanding and Working Effectively With Others: Self-Coaching Questions**

1. What are the benefits of establishing honest and meaningful relationships with colleagues?

2. In what circumstances do you feel most effective: Working alone? Working in small teams? Working with larger groups? If your answer isn't "all," what might your personal demeanor communicate to staff? What steps could you take to increase your comfort?

**Part III: Understanding and Working Effectively With Others: Activities**

1. Make a list of the key people with whom you interact on a daily basis. This list will differ for building and district administrators. Next to each name, write down what you know about what motivates them in their role. List two or three of their key strengths. Note also anything you know that holds them back from fully exercising their responsibilities. What makes knowing this information important? If you struggle assembling this information, how easy will it be for you to work with them effectively?

2. If you're not in the habit of taking your office into the schools, hallways, or classrooms, set up a regular schedule where you can do so. Keep a journal of conversations that you have with students, teachers, and support staff. What information are you picking up through casual conversations? Note how being visible and interacting with individuals impacts your energy—and your relationship with them.

**Part IV: Understanding Yourself: Self-Coaching Questions**

1. What are your top-three values related to work? How do those values currently relate to the work you find yourself engaged in? Where do you have alignment or lack of alignment?

2. Reflect back on an earlier you—the you who stepped into a classroom or administrative office for the first time—and respond to the following:

    Why did I get involved in education to begin with?

    What was I trying to accomplish for my students and for me?

    What impact was I trying to have?

    Why did I want to lead others?

**Part IV: Understanding Yourself: Activities**

1. If you don't already have one, seek out an accountability partner—someone with whom you can have honest discussions about your performance. Set up regular check-ins to establish behavioral goals and explore how you're demonstrating or not demonstrating them.

2. Another important data point could come from those with whom you work. Working with a human resource representative and your accountability partner, consider constructing a simple three- to five-question 360° assessment that you could issue on a platform such as SurveyMonkey. What would you be most curious to hear from them?

## The Bottom Line

It's actually a good thing if your head hurts after answering those self-coaching questions and engaging in the activities. As educators Richard Boyatzis and Anne McKee (2008) argue in *Resonant Leadership*, "Improving one's self-awareness will not happen by accident. This kind of learning requires a commitment to mindfulness: being consciously attuned to oneself, others, and the environment" (p. 29). *Commitment:* You have to be willing to honestly look inside and commit to the regular practice of self-examination, even if the picture is sometimes out of focus. We'll talk more about how to address the results of your self-examination when we discuss contemplative practices, mindfulness, and self-awareness in Chapter 6.

## Try This

News flash: We *all* have that self-critical voice. For some, it's a voice heard only on occasion. For others, it's more frequent. And for some, it's omnipresent. Sometimes, the message is a whisper. Other times, it's a scream. The time and effort it takes to calm the inner critic will vary from individual to individual depending on life circumstances, but the following four steps work for everyone.

1. *Admit it.* You're periodically hearing one or more of Chamine's named voices, right?

2. *Journal it.* Write down *what* the voice is saying, *when* it is saying it, and *how* it is saying it. Doing so gives you specific insight into the type of situation when it's most likely to appear.

3.  ***Name it.*** Give it a slightly disparaging name that speaks to what it typically says. Calling it out in your mind when it shows up (e.g., "Oh, that's just 'Mr. Perfect' yacking away again.") begins to knock it down a peg and isolate it from the rest of your thoughts.

4.  ***Reach for the volume control.*** The inner critic, as its name implies, works *internally*. It's not some external force weighing on you. It's in *you*. The most important step toward calming it is to recognize that *you* have the choice and power here. If its volume is loud, it's because *you* haven't turned it down. Think of it like a radio station that's playing a song you don't care for. Would you sit there for two to four minutes listening to it, or would you turn the volume down? Or better still, would you find a song that you do like?

---

online resources ↖ | Scan this QR code or visit the website at www.shiftingforimpact.com to access the links listed above. |

# Assessing Your Environment to Inform Change

5

## Go Slow to Go Fast

Many leaders' reaction to a new issue is to jump right in to "fix" it. Remember, the brain hates uncertainty, so most any solution can momentarily reduce individual and organizational anxiety. But that reactive behavior often results in addresssing the wrong "it"—the wrong problem—as we see in "A Leader's Story" on the next page.

Whether they're reacting to an immediate situation or proactively looking to improve a certain area of performance in the absence of a three-alarm fire, experienced change leaders know the potential danger of jumping into "solution mode" too quickly. They ensure that they and their team spend enough upfront time studying the situation in all its complexities. They know that this information gathering and analysis will be critical to the clear identification of the problem they are trying to solve. As Principal Donna Schilke observed during our interview,

> There's a wisdom you bring to good leadership that comes with experience—a wisdom that speaks to the calmness you can bring when you realize that most things don't have to be responded to in that moment. There are a lot of times when you can say, let's just sit back a minute, let's get some more information, and let's

## A LEADER'S STORY

Jumping to Conclusions

From an interview with a school administrator

Our standardized test results came out, and one of our administrators immediately overreacted regarding our math scores. They really weren't that bad—there were gaps in a couple of grade levels, but those gaps were then used as the impetus for significant change.

The decision-making process was something like "Look at our test scores. We don't like them," and almost overnight, we ended up changing our math curriculum completely. The curriculum we adopted was way less rigorous and has contributed, year on year, to lower test scores. So that was a process that was a bit of a disaster, and it hasn't been totally fixed.

find out how it was done before or call a few people to get some different points of view.

In short, go slow to go fast.

As we discussed in Chapter 4, the **assess** phase is the first step in the ARC model of successful change. We have seen how critically important it is for the leader to self-assess toward becoming an effective change leader. Now, we will look at how the assess phase plays out at the organizational level. Here, we lay out proven research and data analysis methods as *options* for you to consider and tailor to your needs depending on the complexity of your circumstances. Your "Go, Go, Go!" internal critic's voice may pull you aside and nag, "But you don't have the *time* to do a lot of assessing." Our response to that is, "Do you have time to do the process all over again if the change fails?"

The most critical objective of the assess phase is that your team comes together to develop a shared understanding of what constitutes the real change that's needed and why. Doing so increases the likelihood of buy-in and change success down the road. Former superintendent Karen Rue spoke from experience during our interview when she noted,

When I announced the reading initiative, those within the organization did not perceive the need. I was a solution in search of a problem as far as they were concerned. With the technology initiative, however, they wanted it. They believed it. It was what their kids needed, and they wanted to learn how to do it. Rather than push in as an expert, I listened as a learner on this initiative. I went from "I've got all the answers" to "You've got a vision, and all I've got are questions. Let's figure this out."

## The Initial Assessment

It is quite likely that you picked up this book on change already having the sense that there is a potentially complicated situation you need to address. Maybe you're considering updating a school-wide behavior management program, revising the master schedule to create collaborative planning blocks, reworking arrival or dismissal procedures, creating emergency response protocols, or implementing new instructional protocols.

Whatever the situation, it may initially appear urgent and vitally important enough to do right *now*. If the situation could talk, it might be shouting "Do *something*!" To switch from reactive to proactive mode and avoid duplicating the problem we read about previously, however, that first "something" should be to gather together members of your team to answer some foundational questions. To paraphrase Albert Einstein, "If I were given one hour to save the planet, I would spend 59 minutes assessing the problem, and one minute resolving it."

## What Is "This"?

Take a step back, and look at the current situation within its broader cultural context: Consider the history, people, systems, and beliefs

---

**Provide the Right Kind of Support**

Listen to more of the interview we conducted with former superintendent **Dr. Karen Rue** where she describes the need to listen carefully to her faculty during the district's technology change initiative. Listen for why it was necessary to assemble the right team to determine the real problem they were trying to solve. (Listen via the QR code at the end of this chapter, or click on Link 5.1 at www.shiftingforimpact.com.)

LEADER VOICES

that may be in play. This leadership skill of suspending judgment and looking more broadly at a situation is called adopting the observer's stance. Expert negotiator and cofounder of Harvard University's Program on Negotiation William Ury (2016) refers to this as "going to the balcony"—finding a place of calm where you can hold a wider perspective.

Neuroscience explains this shift in focus as a deliberate attempt to activate the prefrontal cortex so you have access to your executive functions and time to think—in short, taking any emotion of the immediate situation out of the equation. Doing so allows you to continue to be present with the situation while also noticing which aspects of your organization's cultural iceberg we discussed in Chapter 3 might be involved.

### Why Now?

Now that you have activated your strategic brain, ask yourself the critical question "Why now?" What is prompting you to consider making a change now? Often, issues of concern have been present for a long time or are tied to other issues that have been in place for years. So what is happening now that is pushing this need to the forefront? Are you simply reacting to patch a situation, or is this something you need to get in front of proactively with a deeper, more impactful solution? Fully exploring and understanding the answer to this question can help you begin to articulate a rationale behind the need for change *now*. Again, we emphasize Lyle Kirtman's fifth competency (see Chapter 2). The *urgency* to change should be around the matter itself, the situation that isn't adequately supporting your why. For example, "We're not adequately preparing our seniors for the kind of thinking they need to demonstrate in a career or in college." The urgency to address the issue shouldn't hijack the pace of the change initiative, however, because when we jump too quickly with solutions, we often find ourselves in a deeper hole.

### Why?

And finally, as we discussed in Chapter 2, you need to fully explore how any change you're considering will increase your ability to achieve desired outcomes and contribute to the impact you want to have on behalf of those you serve. In short, is there a coherency between this change and others, or is it an isolated event?

## Setting Up the Change Effort

Some leaders can be impatient with process details, but it is critically important to set the organization up correctly for change. Once you have determined that now is the time for your school or district to commit to a critical change effort, you need to create a high-level game plan for the change effort that begins to answer a few key questions.

### What and Why?

Based on your initial scan, articulate the purpose behind the change, being careful to link it back to your organizational why. Phrase your answer here as a question, which the change plan will ultimately answer:

> *How will we, as (organization's name), (description of anticipated change), so that we achieve (the specific outcome) and contribute to (desired impact)?*

For example, a school considering a change that addresses early literacy development might craft an intent question that reads:

> How will we, as Greenville Elementary School, create an approach to early literacy development so that we raise reading levels and contribute to our goal of having students completely ready for middle school?

### Who?

Designate specific people whose time, energy, talent, and expertise might best be devoted to the assess phase. Ensure that team membership cuts across functions and levels of the organization so that you have broad representation and enough staff power to get work done. Assign a driver of the assess effort—someone who will act as a lead project manager of the initiative. Ideally this person can demonstrate a number of talents:

- Understanding of the strategy—the agreed-upon plan of action or policy designed to achieve the desired shift

- Effective ability to implement—the knowledge of how to get done what needs to get done by seeing how the big picture can be broken into smaller doable chunks over time

- Excellent people skills—the ability to use communication and influencing skills as a means to get a diverse, cross-functional team to coordinate

If the change is complex, ideally you should designate 75 percent of someone's time to the project. Doing so is understandably a challenge where everyone in the district already has a "day job." But not designating someone—perhaps a faculty member who can be temporarily relieved of some of their responsibilities or potentially an outside consultant—opens the door to a "pay me now or pay me later" scenario. Without an experienced project manager at the helm of a highly complex project, the ship of change will likely be headed toward the rocks of miscommunication and chaos.

### When?

Decide on a high-level timeline for the change effort. Include placeholder time blocks for the three phases of our ARC model—assess, ready, change—along with an end date by which time your change initiative should successfully conclude to achieve desired outcomes. Build in a cushion in case something goes awry; something usually will. This exercise will admittedly be rough at this point. You're simply trying to gauge the reasonableness of the timeframe. We provide worked-out examples of simple and complex changes at Link 5.2 at www.shiftingforimpact.com.

Think carefully about the other activities that need to occur in this timeframe, and tap into your empathy. Consult with others who understand what heavy lifting is already on people's plates and where they are emotionally. (As we will see in Chapter 6, some changes engender staff resistance because people are simply exhausted from what they see as endless disjointed flux.) Adjust dates to allow for this other work and the likelihood of greater complexity than you envision now.

### Collecting Data

As you begin the assess phase, it's important to view the situation through a wide lens. You want to take in information from various sources and solicit diverse perspectives so as to expand your understanding and open up to more creative and powerful solutions. If the issue you are focusing on is complex enough to warrant a formal change initiative, you'll need to think through aspects and capabilities of various environments that could impact the success of your change.

In Figure 5.1, we demonstrate this thinking relative to our early literacy example where

- the inner circle identifies the key players and capabilities of your internal organization;

- the middle circle identifies external stakeholders and influencers; and, finally,

- the outer circle captures the societal landscape—economic, political, social, and technology trends, policies, and scholarship that may affect the issue you will study.

Mapping out all three layers of this diagram for your particular change will help you decide which elements to assess based on your particular needs.

Figure 5.1   **Scanning the Early Literacy Environments**

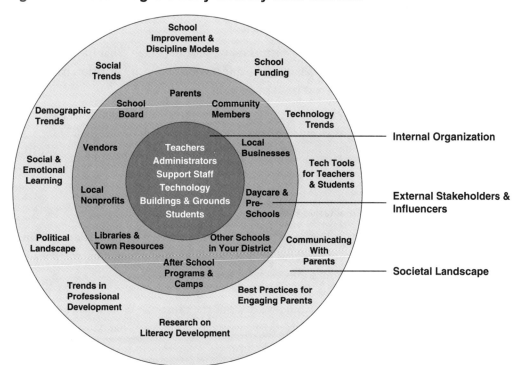

## Use Quantitative and Qualitative Approaches

To assess the true nature of the issue you are trying to address, you may want to consider a mix of qualitative and quantitative research methods. This standard research practice ensures your assessment will reveal both smart and healthy data.

### The Quantitative Picture

Using quantitative methods such as statistics, data analysis, research, and surveys, you will want to get a read on questions such as these:

- How "big" is this issue? How many people are affected? Which groups of people are affected? What percentage are significantly affected?

- What key factors do we measure here? What metrics do we use? What can be understood about the situation based on current performance on these metrics?

- How does our current performance compare with past performance? How does it align with future goals?

- How does this relate to and/or impact the student outcomes we track?

### The Qualitative Picture

Using qualitative methods, such as interviews, observations, community meetings, focus groups, and facilitated discussions, you'll want to consider questions such as these:

- How would we describe the situation? What's the real problem here? What do we worry about most? What do we know? What don't we know?

- How is this situation affecting us? What is it doing to our energy and morale?

- Who is involved here? What attitudes do they bring to the situation? Are some people or systems affected more than others? How might power affect access in this case? What might be compounding this situation that goes beyond what we can control here?

- What are different views of this situation? What assumptions do we have that play into this? Are there competing priorities or conflicting values that are making this complex? How does this relate to people's concepts about "how we do things here"?

- What will happen in the short term if this situation hasn't changed? What will the long-term effects be? How might this keep us from making the impact we intend?

Using this framework, you would plan to scan each level to see how various elements affect the situation under consideration. In Figure 5.2 we see what an integrated set of tools might look like applied to our early literacy example.

### Figure 5.2 Research Tools for Early Literacy Example

| Environment | Research Approach |
| --- | --- |
| **Internal players and capabilities** | • Interviews with elementary teachers, reading specialists, special ed staff, family engagement specialists, and administrative staff<br>• Observations of independent reading, reading pullouts, and tutoring<br>• Comprehensive review of school performance data and in-depth analysis on literacy data |
| **External stakeholders and influencers** | • Surveys of parents<br>• Site visits to local library, after-school program, and preschool<br>• Statistical research on changes in community demographics |
| **Societal landscape** | • Report on new technology options for home–school communication<br>• Facilitated discussion on early literacy trends with staff and community partners<br>• Literature review on evidence-based best practices for early literacy development |

### Key Factors to Guide a Healthy Assessment

When you conduct your scan, you may be tempted to switch into smart mode because you're doing a certain amount of data crunching, which may have you thinking analytically and very right brain. We urge you to deliberately focus on the healthy implications here as well. As discussed in Chapter 1, changes fail because not enough attention was paid to the people leading and executing the change. So you'll want to look closely at the individuals, groups, and departments that make up your school, the people and organizations who support your efforts, and the families and communities you serve. There are three key factors to focus on to foster a healthy analysis: empathy, time, and capabilities and influence.

### Empathy

As you encourage your assess team to learn about the issue, you can promote a healthy approach by looking at the situation through the lens of empathy. Instead of just looking at things from a neutral stance, encourage your team to explore the experiences of the people involved, examining what is going on from their perspectives, getting into their heads, and understanding their thoughts, feelings, challenges, and hopes. One powerful way to do this is to use a tool from the discipline of design thinking called an ethnographic observation.

During such an activity, a member of the design team directly observes the person they intend to serve or the situation they want to improve. They listen to what people say and watch what they do in their environment so as to document their experience. The observer also captures their own insights about the problem that they had as a result of doing the site visit. For example, tailgates on certain SUVs are now activated by waving a foot under the rear of the car. This innovation came about, in part, by observing people in parking lots who were balancing small children and packages.

## MAKING SENSE OF IT

Design thinking is a human-centered creative process for solving problems in that it focuses with intensity on the people who are being served and keeps them at the center as you are designing a solution. This approach was originally used to improve the design of commercial products, but it has now become widely adopted in education and business circles to build better solutions.

*A School Example*—Imagine that you were having an issue with school climate because students and even some teachers didn't feel safe in the hallways. (We'll actually study an example of this very situation in Chapter 7.) Your assess team might do initial interviews with a few representative parents, students, and staff to get a sense of where the issue might be playing out in the school environment. Then you might deploy observers to hot spots—physical areas that have been noted as trouble sites during different times of the school day. There, the observer would take notes about what they see and don't see. Observers could enhance their notes with a few on-the-spot interviews with players at that location and also write down their own thinking and insights about the aspect of school climate they observed.

By focusing on empathy, your assessment will include real-life experiences that show the human details of this issue as it plays out in the current environment. This is vitally important for understanding the meaning of the issue for your people.

### Time

A second factor to examine is how the situation in question has played out over time. As we saw with the "No food in the classroom!" story in Chapter 3, sometimes a leader will approach a change effort as if everyone were a blank slate, when, in fact, some of their staff have had previous experiences that inform the present. As you proceed with your assess phase, you'll want to gather information to see how the situation under consideration fits into the story of your organization over time and helps you project changes into the future.

To accomplish this historical assessment, your assess team needs to collect information and organize it along a chronological timeline chunked into three time periods:

*Past: What was the origin of this issue?*—What happened in the past that caused or contributed to this issue in the broader society, in our community, and in our school? What took place in the past few decades that is relevant? How did we used to think about this? Were there any key turning points? What events took place in the past few years that we need to consider? What highs and lows have we experienced?

*Present: What is the current status of this situation?*—What are recent accomplishments? What are recent challenges or setbacks? What is happening right now? What trends, policies, or issues are affecting this situation right now?

*Future: What do we see emerging on the immediate horizon?*—What do we anticipate happening in the future—in one year, in three years, in ten years? What's likely to happen if we don't change? What could happen if we do?

This time review can be conducted as a facilitated discussion with your assess team and/or a larger group of people representing all three circles of the environment.

### Capabilities and Influence

The capabilities and influencing power of individuals, your school, your external stakeholders, and societal factors, especially regarding ability and willingness to change, make up the third area of focus. As we saw in Chapter 3, high-performing cultures share a number of characteristics, and we can use these as standards when measuring individual and organizational capabilities.

**For individuals, you could assess the following:**

- Are their core values in alignment with our shared organizational values? Do they believe all students can learn, and are their behaviors consistent with this belief?

- If they manage, do they follow the leader–leader approach? Do they take ownership of their work? Do they feel they can regularly use their strengths, talents, and interests?

- How well do they communicate? How well do they collaborate? Are they open, honest, and trustworthy?

- Are they devoted to learning and professional growth? Do they adapt their behavior based on feedback and consistently improve over time?

If an individual's answers to these questions are "No" or "Not well," you may want to consider coaching or replacing that person. If you assign negative responses to many individuals in your organization, you may need to consider adjusting recruiting, mentorship, and ongoing training practices as part of your change effort.

**For the school as a whole, you could assess the following:**

- Does everyone share the same vision? Are we working toward common goals? Is there a sense of shared identity, or are people more loyal to their own groups?

- How effective is the instructional and administrative leadership? Where are the gaps?

- How well do we collaborate within departments and across departments? What kind of relationships do we have with each other? How well do we communicate? Are our communications in alignment with our values?

- Are we open to learning? Diverse and inclusive? Do people feel safe in expressing dissenting views or discussing difficult topics?

- Do we use our performance to make adjustments that improve our outcomes? Are we looking at both short-term goals and long-term health as an organization?

Your school-wide assessment will likely turn up areas of strength and areas needing to be addressed. For example, if the answer to the first bullet is "No," this gap could be addressed later by including a shared mission and vision exercise in your change effort.

**For external stakeholders and influencers, you could assess the following:**

- Have we built active external networks and partnerships? How would we describe these relationships? How do we currently link them to our organizational why?

- What's our level of parent and community involvement? Do we share a sense of identity and community with them? Have we cultivated a culture of transparency, openness, and trust?

If it's initially hard to get a good read on this external assessment, you may not be aware of possible partners or be able to benefit from the perspectives of people with whom you don't yet have trusting relationships established. If that's the case, show your current partners your draft of Figure 5.1. Ask the following questions: "Who else should be involved or consulted?" "Who might have a different take?" "What do you think we might not know?" Probe for both strengths and gaps.

**For the societal landscape, you could assess the following:**

- What are society's expectations for our students? How are current social, economic, and political conversations shaping the educational outcomes we seek?

- What federal, state, and local policies will guide our performance goals?

- What trends in curriculum, instruction, and assessment are likely to affect us? What breakthroughs in technology, science, and education theory are emerging now? Will changes to standards be important to consider?

Regarding breakthroughs and trends, your team can be tapped for their collective intelligence, but like the Apollo program scientists and engineers we noted in the preface, they may not initially know what they don't know. Build time in this assessment process that enables you to uncover unknowns. For example, you might dedicate a small team to collect relevant outside research, hire a thought leader to lead a conversation at a staff meeting, or create scouting assignments for conference attendees. Share what is discovered, and then ask your team what insights they spark.

Gauging capabilities and influence at each of these levels ensures that you are seeing the complete picture and uncovering opportunities. For example, Jonathan Adams, the assistant principal for teaching and curriculum at the International School of Luxembourg, pointed out in our interview that focusing on capabilities was invaluable to his change effort. "Have you spent the time to know your teachers well enough to know that this is within their professional capability? Do you know the professional capital at your school and the culture of your school well enough to make this work?" Answering these assessment questions can help you understand if your people, organization, and external partners are well positioned to make the change.

## Organizing Data and Analyzing the Big Picture

Once you have completed gathering data, you will need to assemble it into a coherent whole. Just as in the data-gathering step, there are a number of ways to organize what you've collected. You could organize key information visually, using a concept map to show how one piece of information connects and relates to others. You could also frame a discussion with your assess team to answer the questions what, so what, and now what?: What did we learn? So what does it mean? Now what do we think this leads us to do? (See Link 5.4 for samples of these two analytical models at www.shiftingforimpact.com.) Or you could use a situation analysis matrix to support your analysis as we do with the literacy example in Figure 5.3.

## Figure 5.3   SWOC Analysis for Early Literacy Example

| | Strengths<br>What are our strengths as an organization, and how can we leverage them? | Weaknesses<br>What are our internal weaknesses, and how can we address them? |
|---|---|---|
| **Internal** | • Experienced K–3 teachers<br>• Effective diagnostic assessment system in place<br>• Strong process for monitoring academic progress | • Poor coordination between classroom teachers and reading specialists<br>• No process for escalating concerns about students struggling with social and emotional issues<br>• Weak home–school connections<br>• Distrust between teachers and administrators |
| | **Opportunities**<br>What opportunities are available to us, and how can we capitalize on them? | **Challenges**<br>What are outside challenges, and how can we mitigate them? |
| **External** | • New funding available from district to address literacy<br>• University research team wants to partner with schools<br>• Largest local preschool open to getting guidance on curriculum<br>• New technology available for parent communication | • State policy change on mainstreaming may disrupt our special ed approach<br>• District considering new diagnostic assessments |

Organizing the information you collected in this way allows you and your assess team to step back and see the full picture, especially noting any patterns and themes. Look for connections between data points and what's new about a situation that you didn't already know. You could go even deeper by working the quadrants against each other when you ask questions such as these:

- How can we leverage our strengths to mitigate these challenges? To capture these opportunities?

- How are our weaknesses preventing us from maximizing these opportunities? From responding to these challenges?

Direct your team to consider what new insights are arising from the experience they had in seeking and considering the data.

## Defining the Right Problem to Be Solved

At the beginning of this chapter, we introduced the idea of generating a purpose statement to help frame early thinking on the change behind the problem to be solved. At this stage of the process, you would want to refine that statement based on the results of your assessment. In design thinking, this is described as the *define* stage—the moment where you consider everything you know about the situation and then define the specific problem you are trying to solve. This prevents you from solving the wrong problem with your change initiative—an all-too-frequent occurrence.

Look back at the results of your assess team's analysis of the information that you organized, especially examining the insights that emerged when your team considered the whole picture. We provide an example of this type of examination, again via our early literacy example:

- Which issues are closely connected, reinforce, or compound one another? What are the relationships between these issues? These types of questions help you understand cause-and-effect relationships. For example, "No process for escalating concerns about students struggling with social and emotional issues" might be related to and even be an effect of "Distrust between teachers and administrators."

- Which one issue, if addressed successfully, would have the greatest impact on all of the others and/or our why? How can this issue be stated even more specifically, given our situation? For example, literacy research may show strengthening home–school connections would result in the greatest impact on early literacy. Greenville's interview data suggested that home–school connections—relationships between parents and their students' teachers and administrators—are often weakest for the most vulnerable students, those who are struggling with social and emotional issues. Therefore, they will address home–school connections in their change effort.

- What is holding this issue in place? What are its root causes? If necessary, use *the five whys* root cause analysis to dig down to the underlying fundamental sources of the surface-level symptoms. For example, "Why (1) are there weak relationships between parents of most vulnerable students and school staff?" Why (2)? "Because they don't know and trust each other." Why (3)? "Because there are only two formal proactive ten-minute opportunities to meet and talk about the child with a different teacher each year, and if the child is struggling, the other interactions with school staff are crisis-oriented." Why (4)? "Because teachers and staff do not have dedicated time to build relationships and coordinate child-centered social and emotional supports and interventions with parents." Why (5)? "Because our school does not have a model for ongoing home–school relationship management for vulnerable students."

- What aspect of this proposed change can we control or most strongly affect? Where should we invest? This helps you focus on the areas of the problem that are inside your locus of control and uses available resources. For example, Greenville Elementary School might decide to feature positive home–school relationships in an integrated school-wide approach to early literacy.

### Refining the Purpose Statement

Now, based on this focused thinking, work to refine the description of change and the outcome or impact desired. Using smart and healthy thinking, push toward definitions of the change in this purpose statement that are both specific and inspiring, realistic and transformational, time-bound and long-term learning focused, technical and people focused.

The refined purpose statement might not be that different from the original statement, but it will be richer, more defined, and more directional. It should feel right to you and your assess team as the guidance for the change you intend to make happen together. It should also be designed to be shared, using clear and energizing language to communicate the purpose of the effort to people inside your organization and even to external partners and stakeholders. For example, based on their assessment, the Greenville assess team might refine their statement to this:

## LEADERSHIP SPOTLIGHT

Figure out the real thing that needs to be changed. Don't settle for just moving the deck chairs around; if you don't find out the root cause of the problem, your boat could still sink.

How will we, as Greenville Elementary School, infuse integrated social and emotional support into our early literacy model so that we raise the reading levels of our most vulnerable students and contribute to our goal that all of our students enter middle school on or above grade level?

## Setting Goals—Linking Purpose to Action

Once the purpose statement is completed, use your assessment to create goals for the change initiative. These goals should flesh out the major elements you must accomplish in this effort. For our Greenville example, the goals for an integrated school-wide approach to early literacy might look like this:

1. Design a collaborative process for coordinating the efforts of our teachers, reading specialists, and special services staff, including time dedicated to integrated planning as well as specific students' progress reviews, and implement the first working version in time for our next back-to-school cycle.

2. Strengthen home–school connections in support of factors in early literacy development, including attendance, by providing real-time communications to parents in print and via a new technology tool.

3. Partner with district and Greenville University teams to develop a comprehensive system of addressing social and emotional wellness, with a special emphasis on providing extra support for our most vulnerable students.

State your goals in the positive, as opposed to describing what you don't want. Go back and look at your organizational why, and attempt to connect these goals directly or indirectly to the objectives arising from the greater purpose and mission of your school or district. Focus on the major themes or clusters of information that came together in the analysis, and make sure that the goals represent each key shift and capture the desired results for each major theme.

## The Bottom Line

And finally—and in our opinion, most importantly—while you crystalize these goals, you must intentionally keep new thinking in the mix. It is very tempting during this moment of pulling it all together to soften the elements that seem risky and default to the way "we always do things." Wanting to do so is understandable because the brain likes to avoid change and the uncertainty that comes with it. Instead, you must push yourselves to make sure that the goals that emerge from this process capture your aha insights. Doing this will help you align your change effort with the bigger picture of the effectiveness and sustainability of your whole organization.

## Try This

1.  What is an issue in your school or district that may require a complex, long-term change?

2.  Given your issue, review the three-ring graphic we introduced earlier in the chapter, and then, use Figure 5.4 to list elements in each ring that may call for assessment to inform your planning. Consider the following questions to guide your thinking:

    - Internal environment: Which individuals and groups are most likely to be involved, and why?

    - External environment: Which organizations represent significant opportunities for partnerships or dependencies that, if not taken into account, could impact success?

    - Societal environment: Which factors are most likely to impact your planning?

## Figure 5.4

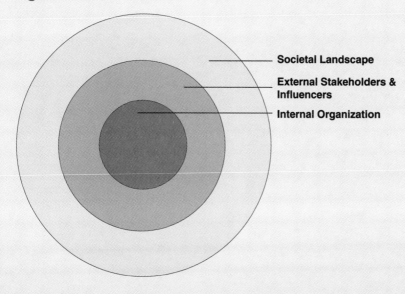

Societal Landscape

External Stakeholders & Influencers

Internal Organization

3.  Now that you've filled out this chart, reflect on the experience.

    •   Look at the chart as a whole. What stands out? What do you notice about each ring?

    •   Which of the elements you listed was expected? Which felt like a surprise? Where do you experience confusion or lack of clarity? Who might help resolve that?

    •   What did this experience make you realize? Which elements seem most critical to assess? How does this help you understand the issue now?

Jot down your thoughts about next steps.

---

online resources ⤳          Scan this QR code or visit the website at
www.shiftingforimpact.com
to access the links listed above.

# Getting Ready to Lead Change Differently  6

Deliberately engaging in reflection strengthens emotional intelligence and builds the leader's ability to behave authentically.

**THE BIG SHIFT**

## A LEADER'S STORY

"Give yourself time to think."

Dave Schuler, superintendent, Illinois District 214
2018 Illinois and National Superintendent of the Year
Arlington Heights, Illinois

When I came to District 214, I knew that I wanted to stay here for an extended period of time because the sustainability of leadership does matter. I wanted to prove to myself that I could put a vision in place and then do it in a way that it lives on beyond me. And so, it took a lot of reflection.

I also finished my dissertation at that time. I went to Madison (Wisconsin), which has a very rigorous doctoral program, and I think if you go through a super-rigorous doctoral program, you learn to listen much more clearly, and I think you learn to ask questions better. I had an epiphany around that time. I stopped focusing on what I was looking to say, and I focused much more on what people need to hear. And those are two very different things.

Also, at that time, I started reading Parker J. Palmer's work. And one of his books is *Let Your Life Speak* where he talks about how if you want

*(Continued)*

(Continued)

to see an animal in the forest, do you run around and scream and yell, or do you just sit quietly and let it come to you? And so often, we're so noisy and directing ourselves with what to do, so I spend a lot of quiet time just thinking, reflecting how might I have done something different. Did I do that right? How should I engage next? My team will always tell you there's rarely a time I use a word that does not have some meaning behind it. So very rarely is something just off the cuff. I'm very, very intentional about the words I use. And so, to do that, I have to spend time really thinking about not what do I want to say but, rather, what is going to be of value to them, and how are they going to hear what I need them to hear.

In the previous story, we witness Dave Schuler's transition from who he was as a leader into one who is an intentional thinker, listener, questioner, and speaker—someone who is well positioned to lead the change process and those making the change. His story is also a perfect example of the point Kimberly Davis offered in Chapter 2: Your authenticity is a reflection of how those you're leading hear and see you.

Reflecting that shift, we move now from the leadership self-assessment we conducted in Chapter 4 into the **ready** phase of our ARC model. (See the preface.) The ready phase helps you, the change leader,

- understand and deal effectively with change resistance,
- begin to overcome any gaps you might have in the areas of authenticity and emotional intelligence—what we'll contend are the twin engines of change leadership success, and
- unleash the wisdom and thought power of your staff to support the change process.

## The Neuroscience of Change: Why and How We Resist Change and What to Do About It

The premise of the ready phase is that once you develop an authentic sense of self, you are better positioned to truly know others and to more effectively manage your interactions with them, especially when undertaking a complex change. Knowing yourself and others also will help you manage the inevitable resistance that comes with any complex change. Let's look there first.

People don't like to change. Harkening back to our human origins, our brains are hardwired to hate uncertainty and to crave predictability. At one time, our very survival depended on it. Step into the unknown, and you enter the domain of the saber-toothed tiger. Better to stay by the cave entrance and the warmth of the fire pit. Undertaking a complex change means stepping away from the fire—the comfort of what's known today—and that often creates uncertainty. Uncertainty breeds resistance that will act like a ball and chain on forward movement.

A number of researchers have spoken to this phenomenon, and their perspectives can be categorized into three distinct areas. Each of these perspectives underscores the point we made in Chapter 1 about why most changes fail and how to counteract the potential for failure: a failure to develop the mindset, talents, and behaviors that leaders and staff need to bring about changes and their desired outcomes; *to focus as much or more on the people leading and executing the change than on the specific change itself.*

## Transitioning From the Old to the New

The transition perspective is best introduced by arguably its most important advocates, William Bridges and Susan Bridges (2016). In their landmark work, *Managing Transitions: Making the Most of Change*, the authors write, "It isn't the changes that will do you in; it's the transitions." And by *transitions*, the Bridges mean the psychological shifts people involved in the change must go through. To fully embrace the new beginning heralded by the change, people must go through a three-phase process:

1. First, they need to be helped to let go of the "old"—the way things have traditionally been done.

2. As people ease out of the "old" mindset, they enter a wait-and-see neutral zone. It's here that they begin to make the necessary adjustments to function fully in the new order.

3. Finally, people fully commit to the new beginning. (Bridges & Bridges, 2016)

It will come as no surprise that most leaders and organizations immediately jump to the final phase—the new beginning—ignoring that they're dealing with people's emotions, habits, feelings of loss, and fears; ignoring that people must first end what they know and are comfortable with before they can tackle something new.

Helping people let go of the old, move into the neutral zone, and, finally, welcome the new beginning is a course unto itself. But we can bottom line your first and most important step this way: If you're not already, you must become intensely aware of others—what they're thinking and feeling, their emotions, their motivations, and so on. Doing so involves stepping out of your skin and into theirs. But the practice doesn't start with them; it actually starts with you and your own self-awareness. More on that in a bit.

What's critical to accept here is this: If you're traditionally inclined to focus more on the technical aspects of change than on the people making the change, you will undoubtedly put your change progress in peril.

## Competing Commitments

One of the more interesting perspectives on change failure comes from Harvard researchers Robert Kegan and Lisa Laskow Lahey (2009), who we first met in Chapter 3 when we touched on the psychological underpinnings of resistance. In their pioneering study, *Immunity to Change*, they write about what they call hidden, or competing, commitments. We created an example of this behavior based on our interactions with a number of administrators.

### A School Example

Dana is a school principal who wants to engage her staff from the leader–leader perspective. She *honestly* wants to build the capacity of others, but upon self-reflection, Dana has to admit that most of her actions run counter to that goal. She finds herself doing a lot of telling, instead of asking open-ended questions. She routinely gives her opinion first rather than asking others for theirs and then listening with intention.

What's critical to note, Kegan and Lahey warn, is not that the Danas of the world are insincere; it's that they likely have a hidden, or competing, commitment to do the opposite of their expressed goal. Dana's honest self-analysis eventually reveals that she feels at risk professionally were she not to remain in complete control. She fears she might even be viewed as superfluous in her role. And most importantly, according to the authors, her commitment to remain in control is *no less sincere*, no less meaningful to her than her expressed commitment to grow other leaders. It's just in contradiction to her capacity-building goal, and thus, it becomes a drag on her change progress efforts.

Not all leaders will immediately be equipped with Dana's self-awareness. If you've openly announced a personal or organizational change goal, observe—or have an accountability partner observe—how much progress you're making toward meeting it. If progress is slow or nonexistent, a hidden competing commitment could be holding you back.

How Dana resolves her situation goes largely beyond our scope here; see Link 6.1 at www.shiftingforimpact.com for a worked-out example. What's important to note here is that the self-aware leader can step back and see where they, or others, are living in a contradiction and putting their change progress in peril.

### Encountering Exhaustion

Authors Dan Heath and Chip Heath (2010) point out that what we often take as staff resistance to change is sometimes just staff exhaustion, which can be brought on by the sheer number of changes we're asking staff to make sense of and manage. Think back to our lengthy list of macro and micro educational initiatives. "What looks like resistance," they caution, "is often a lack of clarity" (p. 15). In the absence of a clear, cohesive story that speaks to the cumulative effect of a number of changes on organizational impact, staff can become frustrated and exhausted. According to Heath and Heath, exhaustion leads to a depletion of the "mental muscles needed to think creatively, to focus, to inhibit their impulses, and to persist in the face of frustration and failure" (p. 12).

If you're seeing crossed arms and pursed lips when you've announced your big, wonderful change initiative, it may not reflect your faculty's and staff's disagreement with the proposed vision as much as it does their physical and emotional fatigue. But the effect is the same: a drag on change progress. Principal Evan Robb, whom we've heard from in an interview earlier, cautioned, "Either you tell your story or someone else will. You want to communicate stories that speak to collaboration and people working together to problem solve and what you value in the organization."

## Shift Your Performance: Developing Greater Self-Awareness

So resistance to change in some form is probably inevitable. But if you are aware of the potential for these reactions to change and if you're in tune with yourself and how your staff is perceiving a shift, you will be in a much better position to navigate the rough waters. So how do you become self-aware? How do you get in tune?

## Contemplative Practices

The road to self-awareness is to engage in something that is very likely to be counterintuitive to every "Go! Go! Go!" leadership bone in your body: to pause long enough to get out of your own way and make sense of what's going on inside and around you—to notice your own activities and behavior and those of others without judgment.

If you're thinking "meditation," yes, but you can pause by any means that allows you to rest in silence long enough to see what's inside your heart, mind, and actions. Such means are referred to as *contemplative practices*, and they can also include walking, cooking, art, yoga, social activism, chanting, visualization, gardening, or swimming. Whatever the activity, the goal is to quiet your mind. If you're like the rest of us, though, you may initially struggle. Quieting the mind in most of the Western world of work runs anathema to its spare-no-initiative, hypercompetitive, sixty-plus-hour-a-week, multitasked, double-booked-for-meetings culture.

## Mindfulness

Using those contemplative practices, we train ourselves to become ever more mindful. We gradually carve out a quiet, safe emotional space that allows us to more fully exercise our senses to bring what's around and inside of us into greater clarity. As we achieve that clarity, mindfulness becomes a state of being where we have greater presence and self-awareness in every situation. We gradually let go of the desire to fix the past or to transport ourselves to the future. We start to live in the present, the now.

### Curiosity

One of the benefits of practicing mindfulness is increased curiosity. As we become more in tune with who we are—our deepest values, our potential—we drop the pretext that things are permanently the way they are and start to consider "Why not?" and "What could be?" We become more comfortable with the unknown. We become more open to discovery.

It is this openness to discovery that unlocks the proactive attitude toward change we spoke of in Chapter 1. If we are open to discovery, we're more apt to look for how we can do things differently—without preconceptions, expectations, judgments, and prejudices—to achieve our desired outcomes and impact. We're more apt to experiment with change on behalf of those we serve, as opposed to being constantly whipsawed by outside influencers.

### Vulnerability

It is this innocence that allows the mindful leader to show vulnerability and admit, "I don't know, but I'm curious to find out." But "I don't know" is also one of the biggest hurdles a leader can face because it represents the unknown, and the unknown always engages our flight, fight, fright, and fear responses. "I don't know" also rubs up against one of the long-held assumptions of leadership: that leaders are expected to have all the answers. So how does the potentially mindful leader break out of this conundrum?

Mindful practices teach us to focus as much on the other as we do on the self. Leadership is about the effect of your actions on others. It's about how you inspire and engage others to work toward desired outcomes and impact. And your authentic actions here will bear wonderful fruit. "People who feel challenged to innovate, learn, and improve exhibit higher levels of engagement than those people who are not challenged. People who are challenged by their leaders are more likely to feel committed to the success of the organization" (Bunting, 2016, p. 88).

In short, your staff has untapped engagement DNA; your people *want* to be engaged and committed. As the mindful leader, you can leverage that desire by nurturing a genuine environment of curiosity, experimentation, and learning. You can start that process by following the advice that Principal Mike Oliver shared in our interview: "I don't know all the answers; in fact, there are very, very few of them that I have—and so when there's a question, I ask, 'How are we going to do this?' and we work together to find out."

---

### Critical Behaviors of the Mindful Leader

**LEADER VOICES**

Listen to part of an interview we conducted with mindfulness author and expert **Michael Bunting** where he describes the "7 Disciplines of the Mindful Leader." As he talks, think about how these disciplines would be especially relevant to the change leader. (Listen via the QR code at the end of this chapter, or click on Link 6.2 at www.shiftingforimpact.com.)

## Authenticity and Emotional Intelligence

We first broached this idea of really knowing yourself when we talked about authenticity being the most important leadership quality you can develop. It's our contention that you can't honestly know and demonstrate Bill George's five characteristics of authenticity without honestly knowing yourself—what lies underneath that exterior of yours (George, 2003). Thus, the road to authenticity is self-awareness—mindfulness—and to become mindful, one must engage in one or more of the contemplative practices we just discussed.

But if successful change is, as we contend, *focusing as much or more on the people leading and executing the change as on the specific change itself*, we need to follow this road a bit further. To fully know others, their motivations, and their fears and to interact effectively with them, you have to possess and demonstrate emotional intelligence (EI).

### Emotional Intelligence

Daniel Goleman, who has authored a number of works on EI and has done much to popularize the concept, outlines its four key skills in Figure 6.1, to which we've added some check-in statements for you (Goleman, Boyatzis, & McKee, 2002). Think of these skills as operating along a continuum of "Not at All" to "Usually." Where do you fall on each statement?

### Figure 6.1  Factors of Emotional Intelligence

| EI Qualities | EI Self-Check |
| --- | --- |
| **Self-awareness**—deep awareness of one's inner emotional life; values; strengths and weaknesses | If I'm totally honest with myself, the person in the mirror has forgotten why they got into this work in the first place. |
| **Self-management**—controlling one's emotions while adapting to change | I have difficulty demonstrating the emotional response that's appropriate for a given situation. |
| **Awareness of others**—understanding of other's emotions and make-up; empathy | I find myself easily distracted when trying to listen to others. |
| **Relationship management**—inspiring, influencing, and developing others while managing conflict | I find it challenging to build mutually supportive connections with my coworkers that can withstand turmoil. |

As Goleman explains, the relationship of authenticity and EI to each other and to mindfulness is critical because of the positive impact those collective behaviors can have on other people. "Relationship management—the crux of effective leadership—at a primal level means managing others' emotions. This requires being in touch with your own emotions and acting from them genuinely" (Goleman, 2018, p. 1).

And so, the converse should be true.

- If you, as the leader, *don't* know your deepest values and emotions and can't control your emotions and

- if you *don't* really know what makes others on your team tick and you can't work effectively with them, then

- you're very likely going to exhibit a temperament and associated behaviors that work *against* your intent of successfully leading a complex change effort.

Again, from our interview with Principal Mike Oliver, "It begins with me. You can't lead others on a path that you're not on. You can't inspire them to become somebody that you're not, so I had to make sure I was living the life I was going to expect everyone else to live."

Let's stop right here. Think for a moment how delicately change success hangs above the pit of failure. Fundamentally, as Goleman concludes, the leader's mood and behaviors—*your* mood and the behaviors *you* exhibit as the leader—drive the moods and behaviors of everyone else (Goleman, Boyatzis, & McKee, 2001). The organization's collective emotional intelligence, then, is the cultural soup in which change will develop and grow or die.

### The Critical Relationship

Clearly, the mindful, authentic, emotionally intelligent leader can't help but have a positive impact on the people executing a complex change. Figure 6.2 highlights the interdependency of these factors.

Contemplative practices increase our self-awareness and mindfulness,

Mindfulness provides the foundation for authenticity,

And authenticity nurtures emotional intelligence.

## Figure 6.2    The Critical Relationship

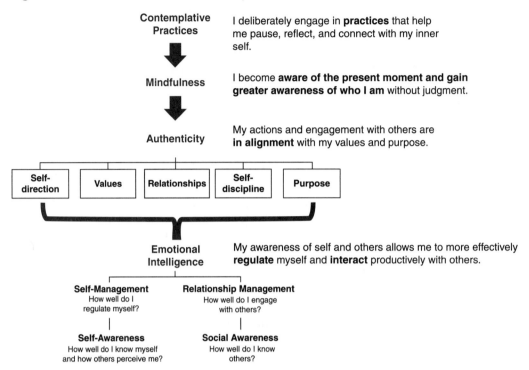

**Contemplative Practices** — I deliberately engage in **practices** that help me pause, reflect, and connect with my inner self.

**Mindfulness** — I become **aware of the present moment and gain greater awareness of who I am** without judgment.

**Authenticity** — My actions and engagement with others are **in alignment** with my values and purpose.

Self-direction · Values · Relationships · Self-discipline · Purpose

**Emotional Intelligence** — My awareness of self and others allows me to more effectively **regulate** myself and **interact** productively with others.

**Self-Management** — How well do I regulate myself?

**Relationship Management** — How well do I engage with others?

**Self-Awareness** — How well do I know myself and how others perceive me?

**Social Awareness** — How well do I know others?

### Readying Your Emotional Intelligence

Our contention is that most of us aren't just suddenly emotionally intelligent or authentic. There is undoubtedly a DNA component here for some, but most of us can learn to demonstrate authenticity and emotional intelligence if we're intentional about it—if we're willing to self-assess and become self-aware of who we really are. If, after reading this section, you sense your emotional intelligence is not where it needs to be to be an effective leader of change, here are some ease-into-it-gently practices you can engage in to grow it.

### Know Thyself

Quick, what are your three most important work values? Achievement? Developing others? Challenge? Recognition? Relationships? And of equal importance, how do you want to actualize those values to meaningfully impact others?

If you hesitated to answer those questions, take some time to dust off your work values and your desired impact—the reasons you decided to be an educator in the first place. You can't authentically live your values at work unless you know them, and merely knowing them without acting on them is like a boat without sails—it's just going to drift with the current and tides.

A sound way to "know thyself" is to construct what leadership consultant Kimberly Davis calls a *super objective*. A super objective is a single statement that encapsulates who you are on the *inside* with the action you need to take on the *outside* to achieve your desired impact (Davis, 2018). It's not a marketing or branding statement. Rather, it's a personal guiding light that brings intentionality to our actions: We *act* in alignment with who we are and what we want to achieve *on behalf of* others. "Act" and "on behalf of" are the operative words here. We are authentic and behave with emotional intelligence. An example would be "I want to unleash the inherent brilliance in people." The super objective doesn't say *how* that objective will be accomplished because there could be many paths to follow. See Link 6.3 at www .shiftingforimpact.com for a template to help you construct your own super objective.

### Pause for Contemplation

What's that? You're curious about meditation as a way to pause? Great, but don't jump into it with both feet! That may sound contradictory to what we discussed previously, but if you haven't meditated before, your initial experience may frustrate you if you overdo it. Instead, carve out as little as fifteen minutes a day where you can sit quietly with no expectations. Get rid of all distractions—no music, lights, or technology. Just. Learn. To. Sit. Quietly. See what comes up for you. Don't try to swat thoughts away. Just notice them and any patterns of thought that emerge.

### Listen. Ask questions. Speak last.

If you're an adherent of the "command and control" belief that you have to have the answers and be the first to speak, turn that paradigm on its head. Start to ask open-ended questions where you don't have a preconceived answer. Don't ask leading questions of staff to get them to come up with your answer. Ask with curiosity, "What do you think we should do here?" "What went well here in your estimation?" "What could we have done differently?" (We'll explore the practice of coaching more fully in Chapter 8.) Listen and watch to learn. Finally, offer your opinion, or make the decision if it's not already clear which way the group should head. See Link 6.4 at www.shiftingforimpact.com for an example.

## Shift Staff Performance: Abandon Commanded and Controlled!

When we're talking about leading and executing large-scale change through a high-functioning team, it's not only your behaviors that likely need to change. When Captain Marquet introduced the leader–leader model aboard the *Santa Fe*, he didn't start with the entire complement of sailors; he started with his five chief petty officers. It was imperative that they be completely bought into the model first because it stipulated a gradual release of control to the rest of the crew. If Marquet failed to get his leadership team's buy-in, the status quo of low performance and limited thinking would have continued on board the ship.

### Aligning Responsibility, Authority, and Accountability

By gradually assuming some authority to act independently, leaders at all levels of the organization must also accept commensurate accountability. That is why Captain Marquet mandated the phrase "I intend to (take *x* action) because (rationale)." It's hard to hold someone accountable or to be accountable without an understanding and acceptance of the rationale behind the proposed action. As Figure 6.3 outlines, this is the essential agreement that fuels leader–leader success.

### Figure 6.3   The Essential Agreement

I have responsibilities.

I gradually obtain greater authority over time to exercise those responsibilities in service of achieving desired results and organizational impact.

I accept that I have accountability for the decisions and actions I take.

Like Captain Marquet, you need to look at your team to see who is willing and able to make this shift, and that ask definitely includes *all* staff members.

An interesting way some schools have gone about developing teacher leaders is to have them help rethink long-accepted structures, such as the monthly faculty meeting. These meetings are usually administrative-driven, one-way announcement and policy shares. In our interview, former principal Donna Schilke shared the following example of how her school shifted the practice.

## A LEADER'S STORY

Giving Up Control

Donna Schilke, former prinicpal, Smith Middle School
Glastonbury, Connecticut

One of the greatest changes we made in our school was allowing teachers to use faculty meeting time to work on programs or changes that needed to be made. They didn't have to all come together just so I could check names off. We might start off with some light refreshments, and then I might give some direction like, "We want you to work on this topic or in this kind of group. Come up with three ideas at the end of your hour and a half, and then turn them into the office and go home." Then, teachers went to their rooms to work. They were so surprised that we would trust them to spend the time working together, and the work that we got out of them was absolutely phenomenal. So our faculty meeting time became very valuable to us.

Moving away from a leader–follower to a leader–leader model and the essential agreement can be a scary proposition, even for those who want a greater role. Authors Liz Wiseman, Lois Allen, and Elise Foster (2013) note three reasons for potential resistance in their book *The Multiplier Effect*, which is a brilliant reflection of the leader–leader concept at work in schools.

### Words Matter

"Aren't we just talking about *delegating*?" staff may be inclined to ask when they hear talk of them taking on the work of the traditional leader. For many staff, delegating has evolved to have a negative connotation (i.e., "You get to move the unwanted work off your desk and put it on mine.").

Instead, in the leader–leader or multiplier world, we're talking about developing talent, recognizing what motivates individuals, noting where their strengths lie, harnessing their energies, and tapping into their wisdom and experience.

Wiseman notes that some staff will look at opportunities to contribute in this new way with understandable skepticism. They may have experienced other leaders who talked a good game but didn't deliver. Or they may have been a follower for so long that their ability to contribute to the fullest has atrophied (Wiseman et al., 2013).

### You Look Like My Leader, but What Did the Aliens Do With You?

The leader–leader and multiplier mentalities call for most leaders to shift, but be advised not to make radical shifts in your leadership style too fast. Ever suspicious of change, staff may be inclined to think you're merely exercising what you were exposed to at a conference or read in the leadership "book of the month club," and they'll doubt your sincerity. As Wiseman et al. (2013) point out, "It can be disconcerting to staff members when their leader leaves one day and reemerges with a complete personality overhaul the next" (p. 182). And just as important, by making giant behavioral leaps, you won't be giving yourself the space to process your shifts and what you're learning.

Finally, in implementing a leader–leader environment that operates according to the essential agreement, use accountability strictly as a learning opportunity, not as a veiled attempt to look for blame.

### Maybe We've Got Some Wrong People on the Bus

In 2001, Jim Collins took the business publishing world by storm with *Good to Great*. After five years of research, analyzing twenty-eight companies, Collins and his team of twenty-one graduate students announced a set of seven factors that *great*-performing companies routinely followed—factors that merely *good*-performing companies did not. (See Figure 6.4 "Factors of High-Performing Organizations.")

School leaders who were usually extremely cautious about applying wisdom from the business world looked up from their desks and wondered whether the same factors could be applied to schools. Soon, articles examining the possibility appeared in *Education Week*, ASCD's *Educational Leadership*, and the *eSchool News*. At least two major educational publishers, Corwin and ASCD, published books applying the *Good to Great* principles to schools. CliffsNotes-type pamphlets supporting book study groups proliferated. Administrators created and made available SlideShare PowerPoints. Jim Collins spoke before various educational audiences.

All of these sources tried to address the provocative question: Could we implement these principles and, in effect, help make merely *good*-performing schools into *great* schools? "After all," as one superintendent questioned, "we know what needs to be done to get results,

## Figure 6.4  Factors of High-Performing Organizations

**Level 5 Leadership**—a combination of drive, modesty, and an unrelenting effort to achieve desired results

**First who . . . then what**—get the "right" people on the team—and in the right places; get the wrong people off the team

**Confront the brutal facts**—take time to understand the difficulties of the current situation

**The hedgehog concept**—recognize and champion what you and the team do best to achieve desired results

**The culture of discipline**—a unique combination of self-discipline and entrepreneurship across the organization; get agreement on the desired results and on the paths to get there—and get busy

**Technology accelerators**—understand that technology is a tool, not the answer

**The flywheel**—desired results are achieved through steady, step-by-step action that builds momentum

*Source:* Adapted from Collins (2001, pp. 12–14).

so why can't we do it?" Maybe, people thought, the principles in *Good to Great* would shed light on what was standing in their way (Collins, 2001).

So many school leaders dove into the deep end of the pool with the best intention to apply the principles from *Good to Great* in schools.

And eventually many of them stopped.

Other outside voices of "change and growth" surfaced as they inevitably do in the field of education, and the culture of internal discipline around leadership, thought, and action that Collins argued so strongly

### Keeping the Wheel of Change Turning

LEADER VOICES

One who didn't stop applying at least one of the principles from *Good to Great and the Social Sectors* (Collins, 2005) is **Deb Gustafson**, former principal of Ware Elementary School in Fort Riley, Kansas. Listen as she describes how she applied the flywheel principle and achieved dramatic results. Pay particular attention to what she determined had to be the all-important first step of the school's flywheel. (Listen via the QR code at the end of this chapter, or click on Link 6.5 at www.shiftingforimpact.com.)

for in the book simply dissipated. And the coherence behind change initiatives that we've argued for dissipated with it. Many educators, pulled by new voices, simply moved on to "the next shiny thing."

That said, one of Collins's findings remains particularly germane to our underlying theme: *People are the turnkey element in productive change.* So understanding "first who . . . then what" or "how to get the right people on the bus, the wrong people off the bus, and the right people in the right seats," Collins (2001) warned, is critical. But what did Collins mean by "right" when applied to education? We offer three points:

*Performance*—The likelihood for strong classroom performance is certainly a factor, but no principal would knowingly hire someone who had a bad track record or who clearly lacked instructional potential. So "right" is more than just performance.

*Attitude*—It turns out that attitude is part of having "the right stuff." Attitude speaks to sharing a commitment to an educational vision or philosophy, having a collegial spirit, and doing whatever is necessary to reach desired outcomes. As Collins (2001) wrote, "In determining the right people, the good-to-great companies placed greater weight on character attributes than on specific educational background, practical skills, specialized knowledge, or work experience" (p. 51).

*Relationship builders*—Researchers Susan Penny Gray and William A. Streshly (2008) showed that school leaders who deliver sustained results excel at building relationships with all stakeholders. Interestingly, this behavior was not one of the Level 5 leadership competencies that Collins identified, but it appears to be particularly important in schools. Strong relationships built on collaboration, communication, and communities of practice can help overcome the isolation that teachers often experience when they close their classroom door. Relationship building is also one of Bill George's (2003) five essential characteristics of authenticity that we spoke of in Chapter 2.

Such relationships can help to

- solidify an outcome-focused agenda on improving student achievement,

- encourage teacher responsibility in making that agenda happen, and

- involve staff in decision making to tap into their thinking and wisdom.

If school staff aren't actively demonstrating these points, one or more of the resistance points we wrote of earlier could be at work. But as Wiseman et al. (2013) note, "You may need to pull some weeds— removing low-performing, diminishing staff members" (p. 182).

## LEADERSHIP SPOTLIGHT

"Get the right people on the bus" to serve as your change-driver support team, including some of your detractors, before you initiate any change planning.

### The Bottom Line

A fundamental truism from innovation science is "The solution is contained within the problem." Relative to our message here, you and your people are sitting with the problem that calls out for change, but at the same time, you're holding the solution. Whenever we work with organizations on a change scenario, we find that there are already people in the organization who have potential insights about why the problem is happening, what the root causes might be, and what the potential solutions might be. From our interview, Principal Evan Robb spoke from experience: "You learn that you don't know all the answers and you can't know all the answers, but if you can tap into the capacity of other people on your team and help them grow as leaders—that's an absolute win–win."

Now, some of the people trying to lead or implement change, including you, may present behaviors that themselves first require changing. And here, there also will be resistance. Lean into and work to overcome that resistance because the rewards are worth it. As we will see in Chapter 7, the brilliance behind actively marshaling your people, as Marquet and Wiseman advocate, is that you leverage the experience, expertise, talents, insights, and strengths of the individuals and groups within your organization and bring their thinking and efforts into the light.

## Try This

Beginning with Dave Schuler's observation at the start of this chapter, one of our central themes is that leaders need to be acutely more aware of themselves and others. They need to observe, ask open-ended questions with curiosity, and listen. We'll introduce the art and science of coaching in Chapter 8, but for now, try this simple reflection exercise.

In a very intentional way, track your interactions with others throughout one or more days by keeping a journal that reflects what you're thinking and how you're responding.

| The situation: | |
| --- | --- |
| **What were my thoughts?** | **How did I respond?** |
| | Spoke immediately? |
| | Decided / answered immediately? |
| | Paused to reflect? |
| | Asked open-ended questions? |

At the end of your self-observation period, reflect on how you're processing information.

- How often did you give yourself the time to pause and think?

- How often did you provide an answer instead of asking for the opinion of another and miss an opportunity to grow their capacity. In general, see what it feels like to follow the acronym: WAIT— "**W**hy **A**m **I T**alking?"

- Ask yourself, "What did I notice about doing this exercise? What felt familiar? New? What does this inspire me to do next?"

---

 Scan this QR code or visit the website at
www.shiftingforimpact.com
to access the links listed above.

# Getting the Organization Ready for Change

7

Successful change leaders unlock people's energy by engaging them in coming up with ideas to shift the current situation into what it could be in the future.

**THE BIG SHIFT**

## Don't Jump the Gun

Once the assess phase is complete and there is a clear picture of the problem to solve, many leaders mistakenly attempt immediately to move directly into change. Doing so is understandable—they want to reduce uncertainty, move their organization forward, and achieve desired results. But taking action at this point is likely to spawn missteps that waste time, energy, and financial resources and quickly lead to organizational frustration. Such actions will lack the power and sharpness needed to succeed. Why? Because the leader hasn't aligned the organization behind the desired change. He or she hasn't properly activated the people who will be charged with delivering the results. And he or she hasn't used the collective wisdom of these people to shape the solution to the problem so that it can be executed successfully. In conducting a comprehensive ready phase, you are being healthy and smart—getting both your people and your project plan set up for change.

## Getting Your People Ready

To ready your people for making a successful change, it's critical to uncover the necessary wisdom—the thinking, beliefs, and skills—within your own organization. It's time to marshal your human resources in the process of inventing what the actual change should look like and how it should be implemented. In Chapter 6, we shared the adage "The solution is contained within the problem." For our purposes here, that phrase means that strong change leaders trust that their staff can invent a workable solution. They're the ones who are closest to the issue itself. Danny Papa, supervisor of social studies, fine arts, and technology education in Jefferson Township Public Schools, New Jersey, noted in our interview, "The role of leaders is not really about the minutiae in the decision making; it's really in the macro things—like how do we encourage teachers to be the decision makers and be the people who are running things?" Marshaling your staff at this juncture helps to actualize the leader–leader and multiplier concepts.

The good news is that if you follow the approach to assess that we recommended earlier, you'll already have started the ball rolling. If your cross-functional team assessed the internal environment, they already interacted with other staff through a variety of research methods (i.e., interviews, focus groups, observations). You've already engaged a broad swath of people who are now aware of a potential change. The assess activities have begun the Bridges's transitions process we discussed in Chapter 6—helping people let go of the old and move into a neutral, curious stance. Now, as you move into the ready phase, you will use that head start to activate others in the organization, enrolling them as active participants in the planning and implementation effort.

## Removing Barriers to Change

The act of marshaling the troops can expose two potential obstacles to change: organizational silos and a weak climate for participation. These obstacles need to be addressed in how you approach getting your people ready, or the potential change will be doomed from the start.

### Breaking Down Organizational Silos

In most organizations, a limited number of people—usually leadership—are devoted to looking ahead at the potential need for change. Most staff are concerned with managing the work at hand and are "held in reserve" relative to engaging in change. This is understandable because modern organizations—profit and nonprofit alike—use the division of labor as a key element of organizing and accomplishing work. Individuals specialize in doing specific tasks, groups of individuals are organized into departments, and vertical levels separate people into progressively higher scales of authority.

If there is not a high level of communication and collaboration, an organization can begin operating within *silos*, where functional areas acting more or less independently of each other create avoidable problems.

- One department's limited focus often results in actions that conflict with other areas and run counter to the larger organizational goals.

- Information, expertise, and best practices available in one department are not shared with other parts of the organization.

- Communication between silos is often strained, and where there is expected collaboration, we can often find competition for stature, attention, and resources.

In education, silos are often represented by the classic dance between teachers and administrators or among multiple grade-level teams, subject area departments, or special education teachers and general ed teachers. As Superintendent Dave Schuler noted in our interview, effective change is going to be nearly impossible if the obstacles that silos present aren't addressed.

## A LEADER'S STORY

Getting Everyone on the Same Page

Dave Schuler, superintendent, Illinois District 214
2018 Illinois and National Superintendent of the Year
Arlington Heights, Illinois

This was an awesome district when I got here, but we had six silos—six high schools, everybody operating in their own silo. And the board was very interested in getting us to work more together. And so, we decided as a superintendent's leadership team, which includes the principals, the cabinet, and me, that we were going to use Marzano's work. It was perfect timing. We started our investigation right when *District Leadership That Works* came out, which at the time was the largest meta-analysis ever conducted on leadership tied to student achievement.

(Continued)

(Continued) So every administrator in our district read that book. We spent probably six months talking about what that meant. Our entire board read that book. And then we had a joint session with our board and all the administrators in our district on why this was going to be our grounding philosophy and what pieces of Marzano's work were going to be critical to us really moving forward.

In addition to having the central unifying understanding that Dave Schuler spoke to, another key way to break down silos and foster cross-organizational communication is by intentionally fostering relationships between people in different parts of the organization and across levels of management. Include staff from all parts of your organization in ready phase activities and feature icebreakers and group work to strengthen bonds. Doing so creates a web of cross-functional and cross-level change agents who serve as activation points, pulling together across silos and generating a sense of community and shared focus that is critical to your change effort as well as your long-term success as a high-functioning organization. In education, cross-functional and/or cross-department relationships could be formed, for example, when team leaders from the middle school and department heads from the high school meet to design a transition program for incoming freshmen. Similarly, the operations manager, the business manager, and the HR director, working with administrators, teachers, and the head custodian of a school, meet to update security protocols.

### Overcoming a Weak Climate for Participation

As discussed in Chapter 3, the culture of high-performing schools is characterized by high levels of collaboration and communication. The presence of a safe, supportive climate in which people expect to contribute to a shared purpose is key to achieving this high level. We've noted a number of times how individuals working within an organization are in an ideal position to know or think through much of what is needed to solve problems and help bring about complex change. In many organizations, however, that intelligence is intentionally or inadvertently locked out. This lockout can happen when an individual doesn't have enough stature to get her or his ideas heard. Maybe she or he is an administrative support person, so her or his voice is discounted. Or maybe a department head fails to escalate information that a teacher has shared. A lockout can also happen when a team or a team leader doesn't want to escalate something they fear might be considered "bad news." Or maybe staff who work directly with parents and are likely to know the most common complaints are not called on to provide input or are not trusted to problem-solve at their level. Sometimes there are already people who are taking action to fix or mitigate a problem in their area of responsibility, but poor organizational communication prevents effective systems-level problem solving.

To overcome this type of obstacle, pay special attention to how participation is facilitated. A natural tendency during this period of uncertainty may be to limit the risk of missteps or miscommunication by restricting who is involved in the conversation. Maybe you are worried that the discussion will involve sensitive information or that making additional people aware of how big a problem is could be demoralizing. But restricting who you include now to people who are already on board may prove counterproductive to overall staff buy-in down the road. Instead, deliberately open up channels for harnessing your people's intelligence and their concerns relative to the proposed change. Create an intentional activation environment—a space where people can share their discomfort, admit to not knowing yet, bring up difficult subjects, tell the truth as they see it, acknowledge missteps, communicate opinions, change their minds, feel conflicted, take a position, and express appreciation and gratitude.

In our interview, Principal Evan Robb described getting his staff ready to envision possibilities when they started the redesign of their middle school library.

> We do a lot of staff reading and book studies. One of the things we did as we were on this journey is spend a whole year reading George Couros's book *The Innovator's Mindset*. Innovation became a very big focus in our building. We had lots of conversations about "What does innovation mean? How do you bring innovation into your life as a professional, and how do you encourage it with kids?" As a principal, you have to set up conditions in the building where people feel encouraged to try these things.

We recommend that when you work on getting the Change Plan ready, as we will describe shortly, you deliberately design these ready activities in ways that encourage participation. This will give your people the security and opportunity they need and want so as to learn, explore, grow, and contribute to change.

**LEADER VOICES**

**Cultivating Change at the Grassroots Level**

Listen to part of our interview with **Evan Robb** where he described how he set the stage for another change initiative: revising the school's grading procedures. Listen for the strategies he used to increase engagement and get people ready to embrace and implement the change. (Listen via the QR code at the end of this chapter, or click on Link 7.1 at www.shiftingforimpact.com.)

Keeping inclusion and participation in mind will help ensure that the ready phase work supports the change *and* ultimately fosters a healthy organizational culture.

## Getting the Change Plan Ready

During the assess phase, you created and refined a purpose statement in the form of a question: *How will we, as (organization's name), (description of anticipated change) so that we achieve (the specific outcome) and contribute to (desired impact)?* You assessed various environments to inform the work.

The next section will outline the steps necessary to build the plan to answer your question. Your staff will help shape the plan with their insights and ideas, figuring out how to create the change given the time, energy, and resources available—all in alignment with your organizational why.

There are four steps in the overall planning process, which we summarize in Figure 7.1 and then detail in the rest of the chapter.

### Step 1: Creating a Vision of the Future

At the conclusion of the assess phase, you decided on goals to focus the change effort. Now, in the ready phase, you must create a vision of what it would look like if those goals for change were successfully achieved. We recommend holding a facilitated meeting in which you and your staff imagine this vision of the future together. Intentionally strive to get diverse thinkers into the planning room with you, creating a multitude of voices in terms of

- inherent characteristics: race, ethnicity, age, gender, ability, and sexual orientation;

- acquired characteristics: experience, skills, geographic location, and language acquisition;

- organization characteristics: roles and responsibilities; and

- thought characteristics: dissenting opinions and different thinking styles and personalities.

### Figure 7.1 Developing the Change Plan

| Step 2 | Step 3 | Step 1 | Step 4 |
|---|---|---|---|
| **Describe the current situation** | **Generate ideas to bridge the gap** | Create a vision of the future | |
| Examine the current situation to figure out the key obstacles holding you back and what you can leverage to make progress toward the vision. | Compare the vision for the future to the current situation and come up with specific ideas to move from where you are now toward your vision. | Imagine what it would look like if the current situation were significantly improved; create a clear, compelling description of this ideal future state. | **Commit to an action plan** |
| | | | Put together a plan and schedule that commits to a limited number of resourced actions you intend to take to bring Step 3 to life. |

It's imperative here to think beyond your go-to faculty talking partners. As Lyle Kirtman's seventh competency suggests, connect to outside intelligence and resources, including students, parents, the school board, community partners, and educational thought leaders.

Here's a suggested process for conducting a vision meeting.

a. Gather people together, and give them a brief introduction to the context. Share basic information, including "givens" or other assumptions. Tell them that you are going to have them imagine the ideal future state, and give them a specific end date by which time the vision is realized.

b. This guided imagery exercise can be used to spark their imagination: Ask participants to imagine getting on a time-traveling train and then stepping out three years in the future. Tell them, "The change has been accomplished, and we are now wildly successful." Instruct them to look around and notice what they see, what's happening, what people are saying, what new things are taking place, what results have been achieved, what's being celebrated, and what it means for students. Bring them back to today.

    c. Have participants write down five specific things they imagined.

    d. Have people share their thoughts, ensuring that every person has a chance to participate. (If there are too many participants to do this individually, you can have people share in pairs or small groups and bring collected ideas back to the larger group.) Write down thoughts so that everyone can see them.

    e. Look at all of the ideas that were shared. Ask people to reflect on their collective picture of the target future. Identify common themes that emerged, and notice outliers. Capture insights. Thank everyone for participating.

Use everyone's interests, passions, and dreams to encourage yourselves to "play big" in the desired future. Creating a common vision is an uplifting and powerful activator.

## Step 2: Describing the Current Situation

Once you have generated a picture of the future, it is important to return to the present state and acknowledge current reality. Without this step, it is likely that the future vision will stay too "blue sky" and seem impractical for the realists on your team. It will help you follow the *Good to Great* (Collins, 2001) advice we discussed in Chapter 6: Confront the brutal facts. This step is often challenging and requires us to be open, transparent, and vulnerable. It can be summed up by these questions:

- If this description of the ideal future state is our target, what does our current situation look like?

- Using data from the internal and external environment assessment, what are the key constraints or obstacles to achieving our vision for this change? What are the root causes for these blocks? What's really holding us back?

- What competing commitments (see Chapter 6) might we have that would prevent us from making effective progress?

- What is working well that we can build on? What strengths and opportunities do we have relative to this vision?

You can do this exercise with the same large group that you used to create the vision if you have a trained facilitator, or you can use your change team as a smaller focus group.

Here, it is critical to demonstrate that vulnerability we touched on earlier. You and your team must be willing to suspend judgment and defensiveness and be willing to open up to what is actually going on. In our interview, Peter McWain, director of curriculum and instruction for the Santa Fe (New Mexico) Public Schools, suggested, "Coming back to what is real is our baseline for growth." Create a summary of the current situation relative to your vision.

## Step 3: Generating Ideas to Bridge the Gap

Once you have clearly articulated the current reality and the desired future, you are now ready to move from the former to the latter. A bridge can be a powerful metaphor for this step, as Tom Marshall, principal of Stony Lane School in Paramus, New Jersey, suggested in our interview: "So here's where you are—now where are you headed? What's next for you? Let's bridge our current practice to our future practice." To accomplish this step, you'll want to hold a meeting where inclusion and participation are most critical. Use the following questions to create your invite list:

- What key team members must be involved? Who will actually have to do the work of this change?

- Who has to manage the actual work associated with the change? Who is in charge of it?

- Which other functional areas will contribute to this project's success? Is there a way to represent every area of our organization?

- How can we include different perspectives, a mix of people we think might be supporters and detractors? Who can represent our diversity?

- Which stakeholders, including those who approve the budget and resources, should be engaged?

- Which thought leaders could help us push innovation and share best practices?

- How can we represent the voices of our students, families, and the communities we serve?

It may initially feel challenging to include representation from all parts and levels of your organization, as well as external partners, when innovating. But as we found out working with one school, doing so can be incredibly energizing and, at the same time, erode the impact of silos.

*A School Example*—A few years ago, a public-school principal retained us to help come up with a plan to improve overall school discipline. Through our investigation, we learned that the places that seemed most out of control—and where many discipline problems originated—were the hallways. We proposed an innovation session in which a representative staff member would get together to generate ideas about how to improve student behavior in the hallways.

### Getting the Right Thinkers in the Room

As typically happens when leaders think about how to solve a problem, the first names proposed were the people the principal normally relied on as part of his management team: his vice principals. When we asked who else should be involved, we received a few more names of teachers who had previously volunteered to develop a discipline code for the school. These teachers represented the "top-of-mind" people— the same folks who are normally the go-to people for solutions. We pushed to make sure this list included a few solution-oriented folks, the cup-is-half-full staff, as well as there-is-no-cup detractors, meaning people who simply felt that "nothing can be done with these kids." Then, we asked about other functional areas involved in managing discipline, and this request added a security guard, an office staff person, a guidance counselor, and a special education teacher. We proposed including representation from the district office, from other local schools, and an expert on restorative practices. We asked about adding representatives from the community.

The expanded and more diverse group produced a much more innovative set of ideas than could possibly have been generated by the original and more limited list of people. And not surprisingly, the proposed solution ideas were better received by the school staff as a whole. Done right, your "Getting Your Plan Ready" and your "Getting Your People Ready" activities go hand in hand.

### Breaking Fixedness

An openness to discovery leads to a proactive attitude toward change. Research on creativity shows that people tend to be "fixed" in their thinking, so traditional brainstorming tends to produce only a limited set of ideas. To get more and different ideas, you need to disrupt people's normal ways of thinking. You can use many methods to break this *fixedness*, such as meeting in a special place, using warm-up activities, introducing an element of fun or surprise, and mixing and mingling different people in groups.

## LEADERSHIP SPOTLIGHT

The brain is hardwired to maintain the status quo; break fixedness by suspending what you know and what you think to be true.

Our strategy to break fixedness for the hallway discipline innovation session was to start by having each participant design a unique name tag that included their name and a picture of an interesting "crowd control" strategy. We then had each person introduce themselves to a partner and explain their symbol and why they chose it. Finally, we had each pair introduce their partner and share the meaning of their respective symbols.

We bridged from this friendly warm-up into the description of the purpose of the meeting by explaining that part of hallway discipline is to think of safely and enjoyably moving students through the halls. This sort of breaking fixedness activity can feel uncomfortable to the more serious-minded participants. If you see this reaction, acknowledge the discomfort, and then, suggest people think of it as adopting a sense of play. Deliberately causing a temporary suspension of normal assumptions allows us to consider new possibilities.

### Breaking the Problem Into Its Component Parts

Since people tend to think of things as wholes, the first step of unlocking creativity is to have them break the existing situation into a list of between eight and twelve components parts. When we focused on hallway discipline, the existing situation was the hallway itself, so we created a component list of items we found in the hallway:

| lockers | lighting | bulletin boards | students | stairs |
| --- | --- | --- | --- | --- |
| floor | doors | bathrooms | backpacks | staff |
| walls | signage | water fountains | display cases | |

### Deliberately Play With the Components

When we run an ideation session, we don't just have people free associate—we use a specific process that provides structure for generating ideas. The ideation tools we use are based on the identification of common patterns within inventions begun by Genrich Altshuller

(TRIZ) and refined into an innovation method called systematic inventive thinking (SIT). In this system, you deliberately play with the components of an *existing* product, service, system, or process using one of five tools—subtraction, multiplication, division, task unification, and attribute dependency—to produce novel thoughts (Boyd & Goldenberg, 2013). This is not brainstorming in the ether world. It's innovating against what you already have. It's innovating *inside* the box.

To start the ideation session, take the list of the main components of the existing situation, and write each component on a separate index card. Next, give each person or pair an index card with a component. Have them suggest answers to the questions for one or more of the tools:

*Subtraction*—What if we eliminated this component? What if we partially subtracted it? What might be useful about what's left?

*Multiplication*—What if there were multiple copies of this component? What different job could each copy help do?

*Division*—What if we changed the order or sequence of this component? How could moving this component change the situation for the good?

*Task Unification*—In addition to its normal job, what if this component could help us accomplish the change we want to see?

*Attribute Dependency*—How might this component change in different circumstances or situations (time of day, season, presence or absence of someone or something, in or out, high or low, new or old, etc.)? What could the benefit of this new "if/then" relationship be?

**LEADER VOICES**

**Innovating *Inside* the Box**

Listen to our two-part interview with **Amnon Levav**, chief innovation officer of SIT (Systematic Inventive Thinking), where he reviews the firm's "function follows form" innovation process. Listen for why innovating with constraints and manipulating what you already have yielded better results than trying to innovate out of thin air. (Listen via the QR code at the end of this chapter, or click on Link 7.2 at www.shiftingforimpact.com.)

Encourage your people to generate as many ideas as possible. Don't stop when you've come up with one since the most powerful ideas are usually two or three rounds in.

In our school situation, we used these ideation tools to generate ideas about improving hallway flow and discipline. One pair coming up with ideas about signage thought it would be useful to have the normal signage in the halls and also have personalized signs that showed which teachers are in which rooms to limit students from needing to wander the halls in search of teachers who moved classrooms. Another pair suggested grade-specific stairwells stationed by teachers who know students in that grade. A third planned to reduce congestion at water fountains by installing dual-fill stations for water bottles. See Figure 7.2 for additional examples of ideas that were generated.

By the end of the session, the team had generated more than thirty ideas to improve hallway discipline.

## Figure 7.2   Examples of Innovation Tools Sparking Ideas for Improving Discipline

| Innovation Tool | Ideas to Improve Discipline in Hallways |
|---|---|
| **Subtraction** | *(Subtract Door)*<br><br>**Pocket Doors:** In high-traffic areas, subtract the existing swinging doors that slow down people's movement, and replace them with pocket doors that can be opened during passing periods. |
| **Multiplication** | *(Multiply Bathroom)*<br><br>**Rest Room:** In addition to regular bathrooms, create a specific room where students can go when they need to rest or recover themselves. It could be a lounge, discussion space, or just a place to have a mindful moment alone to recoup. It lessens hangout time in bathrooms. |
| **Division** | *(Divide Students)*<br><br>**Staggered Dismissal:** Create a different time for dismissal that is staggered for the seventh and eighth grades to lessen traffic jams and reduce conflicts. |
| **Task Unification** | *(Give Another Task to Wall)*<br><br>**Restorative Comments:** Design a wall space where students can post and view relationship-building comments (praise, apologies, acknowledgments, affirmations, etc.). |
| **Attribute Dependency** | *(Create Dependency Between Lighting and Time)*<br><br>**Smart Lights:** Lights start blinking thirty seconds before the late bell goes off, so students receive a nonverbal signal to get into their class on time. |

### Focus on Benefits First . . .

As ideas are occurring to your team, make sure to focus on the benefits first. Have people answer these questions:

- What could be useful, helpful, and beneficial about this?
- Who might want this?
- What can this allow us to do that would be good?

Notice which ideas have a "charge," or create an instant ripple of response in the listeners. What do people laugh at because it seems silly? Surprising? Weird? What gets everyone to lean forward in their seats? What benefit seems to be the most powerful or intriguing? What's energizing? What's really new or unusual? What's cool? The more your people can identify what the benefits of the idea are, the more likely you are to stick with the idea long enough for it to gel. If you get excited about the potential of an idea, take the time to clearly describe how it could help address the situation under question.

### . . . Then Acknowledge Challenges

After you have a clear sense of what could be beneficial about a concept, then you are ready to think about what makes it challenging. Instead of feeling like people's resistance is getting in the way, encourage everyone to see it as an opportunity to learn more that will allow you to adapt ideas and make them stronger. Articulate the real challenges—allow your team to explore what makes the idea challenging to fully execute.

- What makes this cost too much, impractical, far-out, or not likely to be adopted?
- What would be a reason that people would reject it?

The more you can understand this, the better you can see what to do next.

### Massage Ideas Until They Are Doable

Once you have identified a high-benefit idea, rework it to address any challenges you've noted. To help you adapt, you can ask these questions:

- How could we still get the benefit of this idea given our constraints?
- What if we execute the idea in stages?

- Might we limit the idea to a smaller scope?

- How could we do a partial idea?

- Can we marry this idea up with an earlier idea from our ideation list to make it easier to accomplish?

- Could we use a "flavor" of this idea to spice up a simple alternative?

- Does this idea make us think of other new ideas that are more viable or feasible?

When adapting an idea, we encourage teams to focus on the heart of what makes the idea special. As Amnon Levav, the chief innovation officer of Systematic Inventive Thinking, cautions, "Limit rather than dilute"; while keeping the essence of the idea intact, look for ways to cut down the scope, scale, or timing to make it more feasible to do. Take note of any new possibilities that emerge from this exercise. Developing your adapting skills is almost more important than your ideation skills. When the spark of inspiration has been adapted into a viable proposal, then it is ready to add to an ideas list.

The hallways innovation team decided to adapt one promising idea they called Smiling Steps. The first version of this idea called for all teachers to be stationed in the halls at key locations at each passing, greeting students by name and connecting with them to build positive relationships. After thinking through how to achieve the heart of this idea in a practical way, the staff chose to limit it by picking the busiest passing on the rowdiest day—Friday, fifth period—and by creating a special Friday Smiling Steps Passing. After making this adjustment, the innovation team felt it was ready to share with their whole school at an upcoming staff meeting.

At the conclusion of an ideation session, you will need to decide which ideas you want to pursue. It might be obvious which ideas merit further work, or you may need to use a decision-making tool. Sometimes, we quickly assess which ideas rise to the top for everyone by allowing them to vote on the options. Other times, we use a score-card to rank concepts or check in with stakeholders to see which ideas

## LEADERSHIP SPOTLIGHT

Focus change efforts on the heart of the idea; limit rather than dilute.

most closely align with organizational strategy. (However, don't throw anything away; keep the rest of the ideas because you might pull from an ideas list at some point in the future.) Once you know which ideas to pursue, you can use your people to suggest next steps.

### Step 4: Committing to an Action Plan

The final step of the ready phase is to pull all of your thinking together and convert it into an actual plan of action. This should be written out as a readable, shareable, approvable document—a high-level plan that places your innovative ideas into a reasonable time frame so you can commit to the specific, targeted actions you intend to take to make the change. Here are guides for developing such a plan:

a. **Think about timing:** Go back to the initial thinking about the change process and timeline that you sketched out in the setup part of the assess phase. How long will the implementation of this change take? Key dates? Desired end date? What other activities will occur during this same time period that need to be factored into the organizational timeline? Do you need to break this implementation effort into phases, allowing for short projects and longer-term plans that align with a school year or budget cycle? How much time is built in for learning from experiments and stepping back to regroup? Allocate extra time if this change is high risk and sensitive or requires partnerships and community engagement.

b. **Link to your why:** Review the vision, blocks, direction, and ideas you have created in the ready phase. What do you need to do to make significant, innovative progress toward your vision in alignment with your organizational why?

c. **Commit resources:** Consider how much staff time, energy, and resources you can bring to bear to make this change. What resources will be needed? What's the high-level budget? Are there specific people you must assign? Any outside resources that must be secured?

d. **Create a project plan:** Map out the key tasks and subtasks associated with this project, and assign due dates and owners to each task. What are the major steps to get this change done? In what order should each task be accomplished? What are the dependencies? Who will oversee this? Who will be accountable for each task? By when must each task be done?

e. **Draft a formal document:** This doesn't have to be long, but it must be clear so that you can share it with your stakeholders, such as district administrators and the board. (See Link 7.3 for a one-page model of an action plan at www .shiftingforimpact.com.)

f. **Refine until it can be approved:** Get input on your draft plan before it is finalized. Who needs to weigh in here? How can we use their feedback to make the plan more feasible? Who must approve it?

Make sure to get approval for the plan from stakeholders so that it receives official organizational commitment. If full approval is not possible, then see if you can get buy-in for the first phase of the plan. Once it has been approved, share a summarized version of the plan with your staff so they can see the results of their participation and feel ready for the change.

At the conclusion of the ready phase, pause for a moment, and appreciate the power you have harnessed. Take time to witness the wonder of activating your people this way, and express your gratitude for their focus on change. Once you are ready, you can successfully deploy the people you have marshaled into battle—moving into the change phase.

## Try This

Breaking fixedness opens us up to new possibilities, activating our creativity and encouraging a sense of play. Think of something that you'd like to see in a new way, such as a problem you've encountered, a familiar location you've become blind to, or an achievement you'd like to build on. Take a photo to represent that situation.

Now, make an appointment with yourself to spend a specific block of time on ideation. Grab a notebook, a pen, and the photo, and go to a different environment than you usually work in—a fun coffee shop, a quiet place of beauty, a walk in nature. Examine the photo carefully, writing down a list of the components you see. There is no need to be literal; use the photo as a jumping-off point to consider separate aspects of the situation on which you are focusing. Number your component list.

Now, deliberately play with each of the components on your list. Run thought experiments by:

- crossing a component off,
- combining two components into one,

- reversing or inverting the component, or

- connecting the component to something you see around you in your new environment.

For each thought experiment, imagine what might be good about this. Write down new ideas that occur to you. Notice new thoughts you have. Capture insights that arise from this experience. You will be amazed by how a short exercise like this can shift thinking and unlock brilliance.

 Scan this QR code or visit the website at
www.shiftingforimpact.com
to access the links listed above.

# Implementing Organizational Change 8

Demonstrating two key leadership behaviors during implementation—
experimenting with what works and coaching for performance—
can significantly improve the likelihood of achieving change
success.

**THE BIG
SHIFT**

In the ready phase, you worked to get yourself, your people, and your plan ready for change. Now we arrive at the final phase of the ARC model: **change**. In the change phase, you shift into motion, taking action to transform your organization.

Previous chapters examined change from the perspective of the leader and the organization separately so that we could provide a deep dive into the critical concepts that underlie each. In this chapter, we view the leader and organization together as partners in the dance of change.

It will come as no surprise that we're going to advocate that leaders and the organization as a whole spend a very high percentage of their time focused on the people doing the actual implementation. Our hope is that by this time, you're nodding along in agreement with the concepts that support this focus: leader–leader, the alignment of responsibility > authority > accountability, and healthy balancing smart. In this phase, we recommend that you do the following:

1. Accelerate out of the gate.
2. Find what works.
3. Coach for performance.
4. Finish strong.

While we provide pointers for the first and last ideas, we'll focus most of this chapter on the two middle ideas since they keep our attention on both the smart and healthy aspects of the change process.

## Accelerate Out of the Gate

It's really critical when beginning the change phase to initiate a few key actions so that implementation gets off to a strong start.

### Get the Momentum Going

First thing to do? Get the ball rolling. Look at the first tasks in the plan and ask, What's an easy action can we take to get something concrete accomplished? We call this a *quick win*. We recommend that you identify at least one quick win and focus on completing it immediately. This will allow you to celebrate the beginning of the change, demonstrating that it's really happening, so as to create a sense of excitement in your staff. It'll get that *Good to Great* (Collins, 2001) flywheel turning.

### Devote a Dedicated Team

One critical success factor at the start of the change phase is to empower a team of people who can do the heavy lifting required to get the job done. The caution flag here is that the kind of people needed for this effort may be the ones you often rely on to accomplish other critical activities. They all have important "day jobs," and it may be difficult to free them up enough to allow them to work on some other big initiative. We get it; this step is hard. But if you don't figure out how to establish a strong, trusted team, you can kiss all your previous work toward this change good-bye. Here's what we recommend:

- Create a dedicated cross-functional team of people committed to working on this effort.

- Ruthlessly clear other work from their plates where possible.

- Continue with the same project manager you identified in the assess phase who will call meetings, coordinate work, keep track of progress, and escalate needs.

- Schedule intensive time blocks for this team to have collaborative working sessions so they can get the focused tasks done.

In the spirit of leader–leader, support the team to own this work, organize themselves, identify what they intend to accomplish in the limited time they have, and use their knowledge, skills, talents, and inspiration to achieve their target outcomes.

## Mind the Rest of the Ship

In addition to designating a team to implement the specific change, you will again need to "go to the balcony" and keep the wide-angle view of other critical school or district activities. Depending on its complexity and timeline, you might otherwise be inclined to focus most of your attention on the change process. The danger in focusing there is that staff not involved in the change can feel left out and react in some less-than-healthy ways. Human nature is human nature. Those standing on the sidelines witnessing a complex shift may feel jealousy—that their work doesn't matter as much as what's going on with the change team. In the worst cases, you could see sabotage and chaos. This is the perfect opportunity to reinforce the *essential agreement* we discussed in Chapter 6, where you align responsibility with authority and accountability for *all* staff. In short, set clear expectations for the behavior of your change team and its immediate leadership and for others not directly involved in the change.

## Find What Works

Like the spirit of play you deliberately invoked during the innovation step of ready, the change phase is best served by promoting a sense of experimentation. Even when adopting an evidence-based model that has been tested and proven in other schools, you will need to find what works given your unique situation and strategic goals. Encourage the team to take action, not along a rigid path but along an experimental one. Coach members to learn from early results and refine the implementation accordingly. Use any early wins and learnings as opportunities to grow and celebrate.

In Chapter 3, we heard from Dr. Richard Gonzales about his efforts to revise UConn's administrator preparation program. Here, he continues from our interview, "You can't just give folks a blank slate and ask them to go for it. But on the other hand, you can't set too rigid a course. I make it clear what we're trying to accomplish, and then, I let people operate. The more I do this, the more I'm inclined to continue working this way because the best answers come from the people who are doing the work."

## A LEADER'S STORY

"It doesn't have to be all or none."

Donna Schilke, former principal
Smith Middle School, Glastonbury, Connecticut

Don't let things like schedules and bells limit you. Pilot things. Piloting is a wonderful way to make change. For those who are really resistant or for a change that is really difficult, pilot it. If you have a high school, certainly your freshmen are new to everything, so you can do something brand new with them. This has been done successfully with block scheduling. Or do something different with a certain grade level or class. Look at a smaller way to pilot it, and get feedback after six months or a year. It doesn't have to be all or none; that all-or-none mentality is very limiting.

### Experimentation

Since the change phase requires you to do new things, there is always risk—the very real possibility that something that you try will fail. Therefore, when approaching this situation, consider how you can set it up less as an all-or-nothing attempt and more as an experiment. Calling the new activity an experiment connotes that it is a limited test of a potential solution with no guarantee of a successful outcome. In *Turning the Flywheel*, Jim Collins (2019) describes this approach as "fire bullets, then cannonballs." First, he advises, you deploy a number of small, inexpensive, low-risk experiments, or "bullets," so you can see what hits. Then, you can calibrate your targeting so you can invest big with a "cannonball" and be more sure to successfully make the impact you intend (Collins, 2019). Like a number of the leaders we interviewed, Donna Schilke recommended, "Let's pilot this and see what happens."

### Reflection

To get value from experimentation, you also must lean on that habit of pausing to reflect that we discussed in Chapters 1 and 6. Reflection is where the actual learning happens. At the conclusion of each experiment and at regular intervals during the change phase, you and the dedicated change team should pause and reflect on progress to date. Invite multiple perspectives to consider the following:

- What happened? Are there any gaps between what we set as our goal for this point in time and what we are achieving now?

- What seems clear? What is confusing or conflicting?

- What significant issues or patterns are surfacing here? What key implications does this have on our change project goals? For our shared why?

- What does this suggest for our next experiment? What should we do now as a result of our discussion about this?

The shared insights that emerge from this analysis drive collective action toward desired results. This pause for reflection has a greater impact beyond just directing future actions—it is actually the most effective method of "cultivating leadership behaviors in everyone" in an organization.

### Iteration

Emerging as a core principle from the discipline of design thinking, *iteration* is the idea of developing new products, services, processes, or approaches by starting with a simple version and then building on what you learn from that to design ever more sophisticated versions until you achieve your desired outcome. In our interview, Richard Gonzales talked specifically about this idea when explaining the process of redesigning the administrators' program at UConn. "You can't keep working on it forever. At a certain point, you've got to call it and say, 'Here's what we're going to go with.' So I'm fine with 'it's good enough for now' because I know we're going to make adjustments, and they'll be better in second iteration and even better than that in the third iteration."

Depending on the complexity of the change, you may want to build in rounds of deliberate iteration. Start small with a simple version of your experiment—a small pilot—and get feedback and reflect on what you learned. Then undertake another version—a larger pilot—that's more developed and gives you even more realistic feedback.

## LEADERSHIP SPOTLIGHT

Date change strategies before you marry them. Make the potential change real by modeling it, testing it, sketching it, and telling stories about it. Give people a taste of what could be.

After several iterations, you can formalize the solution you have per-fected and roll it out for full implementation.

## Coach for Performance

Let's now dive deeper into the idea of reflection that we've spoken of a number of times in the book. The change process is an engine in constant need of attention. As we stated in the preface, our change process is not linear. Along the way, the team will encounter speed bumps of various sizes—speed bumps that have to be navigated to help bring about long-term success. So, along the way, it's essential to hold regular discussions where the work in progress is reviewed in both one-on-one and group settings. An essential leadership behav-ior to ensure that your people leave such check-ins feeling connected and having greater clarity on immediate next steps is coaching for performance.

We first introduced the importance of coaching back in Chapter 2 when we outlined the six leadership styles of the resonant leader (Goleman, 2002). "Coaching," according to one definition, "is the essential tool for optimizing people's potential and performance" (Whitmore, 2009, p. 95). Let's unpack this definition to fully appre-ciate its power:

- *"The essential tool"*—There are other tools for raising people's potential and performance, but coaching is the one that is "absolutely necessary and indispensable" according to the definition for *essential*.

- *"Optimizing people's potential"*—Coaching has the power to move people's performance beyond what they or others thought capable.

- *"Optimizing people's performance"*—Coaching can deliver results that exceed expectations.

Sounds amazing, yes? So why don't more leaders become *coaching* leaders? We offer three reasons:

1. They think the practice will take too long—better to just tell people what to do and move on. And besides, directing and telling has traditionally been expected of leaders.

2. They're uncomfortable with the idea of coaching because it deals with people and ambiguity—the healthy side of the work. Our brains, as we've pointed out before, are

uncomfortable with ambiguity; they crave certainty. Directing, telling, and ordering all serve to create "certainty" in the leader's mind.

3.  They don't know how.

Pleading with you here that "No, honestly, coaching doesn't take that long" or "You won't be uncomfortable, we promise" won't change your behavior if you tend to stand behind numbers one and two. Exposing you to tools and letting you explore them at your own pace may. So let's focus on number three.

## Ask and Listen

Many leaders who are understandably reluctant to coach feel that it's something they can't do because they weren't trained or certified as a coach. In our interview, Michael Bungay Stanier, author of *The Coaching Habit* (2016), points out that principals, superintendents, and other administrators might be thinking "I'm not even sure what you're talking about when you say coaching" because it's one of those words that comes loaded with history, assumptions, and presumptions. Bungay Stanier offered a simple, potentially tension-reducing response to that confusion: "Try to behave more 'coach-*like*.' And by that I mean, can you stay curious a little bit longer? Can you rush to action and advice giving a little bit more slowly?" So experiment here. In both informal and formal settings, approach discussions with staff with curiosity, without judgment, and from a position of personal vulnerability.

## Curiosity

If there is one bedrock behavior the coach administrator needs to cultivate, it's curiosity. It's powered by an authentic desire to learn and to learn more. To fuel your curiosity, avoid asking questions that only yield "yes" or "no" responses, as they don't move the conversation forward without asking another question. Instead, ask open-ended questions beginning with an emphasis on the *what* and *how*. Consider these examples:

- "How are things going?"
- "What's going well?"
- "What problems are you encountering?"
- "What do you think we should do here?"

- "What's your concern with doing that? Not doing that?"
- "What information might you be lacking to make the decision?"
- "What are the critical interdependencies with other groups right now?"
- "What solutions are you putting in place?"
- "How might we resolve that problem differently if it were to come up again?"
- "How can I help?"

And the best coaching question of all? Bungay Stanier suggests it's the AWE question: "And what else?" Asked one or more times during a conversation, "And what else?" serves to keep you being curious and ultimately helps the person sitting across the table peel back the layers of the onion and get at what's really going on (Bungay Stanier, 2016).

## LEADER VOICES

### Stay Curious a Little Bit Longer

Listen to our interview with **Michael Bungay Stanier**, author of *The Coaching Habit* (2016) and founder of Box of Crayons, an organization that promotes coaching as the essential leadership behavior. Listen as Michael recounts the five layers of resistance to coaching—and how he counters them. (Listen via the QR code at the end of this chapter, or click on Link 8.1 at www.shiftingforimpact.com.)

Two other points about curiosity and coaching are worth noting here.

### Reframing

It's important during a coaching session to check in periodically with the staff member to make sure you're understanding what she or he is saying. *Reframing* sounds something like "Great, let me see if I've got your drift here. What I hear you saying is _____. Do I have that right?" Reframing also communicates to staff that you're an active listener.

### Testing

Coaching isn't just a one-way street. You can use part of a coaching session as an opportunity to test one of your own ideas and get valuable staff input. The key in doing so is to carefully phrase your idea so it doesn't appear that all you're really looking for is a rubber stamp. For example, "OK, here's something I'm wondering about. What if we were to _____?" Or "I don't have the details worked out here, so let me get your reaction to the idea. What about this idea might have benefits? What might the drawbacks be?" Here's the bottom line: Never ask questions like this unless you're totally open to staff input. Legitimately using that feedback to shape your idea is a great way to build trust in the coaching process.

### Without Judgment

Avoid leading with *why*-type questions as they can unintentionally imply displeasure or criticism (e.g., "Why did you do *that*?" or "Why do you like *that* option?"). Approach the conversation with a completely open mind, devoid of preconceived notions about causes or solutions. Position yourself to be surprised.

## LEADERSHIP SPOTLIGHT

Coach out of curiosity and vulnerability. Don't be afraid to say "I don't know. What do you think?" Move away from having to have *the* answer. Let coaching inform you about you as much as it informs you about others.

### Vulnerability

As we've discussed before, many leaders assume that they are supposed to have all the answers. Leading from that assumption will doom a leader–leader environment from the start. But just switching off that practice will be a challenge, as you may have *an* answer right on the tip of your tongue. To coach effectively, you have to avoid giving the impression that you merely want people to come up with the answer you may already have in your head. That is playing "Bingo!" and the common staff reaction is to feel resentful and manipulated. If your staff is not used to working with you in a coaching environment, gradually introduce coaching questions into the discussion, preceded with "I'm honestly curious here" or "I don't know, what do you think?" Approach the conversation with the belief that any answer you have might not be the only answer. See Link 8.2 at www.shiftingforimpact .com for a sample coaching session.

### The Benefits of Coaching

Informal and formal coaching sessions can yield a number of benefits.

#### Hold Individuals and the Group Accountable

The overarching purpose of a coaching session is not to play "Gotcha!" but to gain clarity around the critical question "How well are we doing to reach our desired outcomes and impact?" Listen for resistance, understanding, speed bumps, thoughtfulness, ingenuity, and energy. And the key is to listen with your eyes as much as you listen with your ears. Watch the body language of the person you're coaching, and become aware of his or her tone of voice. What do both reveal about the state of affairs?

Yes, coaching sessions can be accountability sessions, but we're not looking for blame or punishment here. Instead, use the coaching session as an opportunity to grow the person or team sitting across from you with "What did we learn here?" or especially "How might you do things differently in the future?"

#### Promote the Leader–Leader and the Multiplier Mentality

Use the coaching session as an opportunity to unleash the thinking of the person or team sitting across from you. Explore solutions to problems with "What would you recommend here?" and "Interesting. What's your rationale for suggesting that?" That last question gives you the opportunity to gauge the way they think and where you might need to provide some quick redirection. In asking these open-ended kinds of questions, you're promoting staff ownership, and staff ownership breeds trust and optimism.

**LEADER VOICES**

#### Listen for Brilliance

Listen to part of an interview we conducted with **Steve Paul** where he outlines the goals, steps, and benefits of a performance acceleration meeting. Listen for why he puts a heavy emphasis on behaviors that affect the healthy side of his business. (Listen via the QR code at the end of this chapter, or click on Link 8.3 at www.shiftingforimpact.com.)

#### Accelerate Performance

Develop a regular practice of formally or informally coaching individuals and teams. Informal coaching may involve asking questions as you casually interact with staff on building walks. Formal coaching can take place in what our colleague, Steve Paul, referred to in our interview as *performance acceleration meetings*—weekly sit downs that can take as little as fifteen minutes. Explore this approach with the "Try This" steps at the end of the chapter.

Choose not to coach, and don't be surprised when issues go unresolved, energy drains from the team, and change progress is hampered.

### Self-Coaching

As we argued in Chapter 6, if you don't stay in tune with yourself, you're setting yourself up to have problems managing and interacting with others. In the heat of implementation, your old, nonproductive, non-people-focused behaviors may reemerge. You may perhaps suddenly start to focus only on smart-side activities because they're what you know. You may also get into your own head and invite your inner critic to the table, blaming yourself for what may actually be expected consequences of change. When those charged with actual implementation turn around to get your emotional sustenance—and if the change is long term and complex, they will—you won't be there for them.

Carve out dedicated time to slow down, pause, and reflect. Check in with yourself on the behaviors you're observing in yourself and others. If you don't already have one, navigate the change with an accountability partner. Choose someone who can observe you and call you on your behaviors, good and bad. Set up a regular opportunity to download and reflect.

## Finish Strong

As you work through the change phase and approach the completion of implementation, we recommend that you take several key actions to make the process more effective and ensure lasting results.

### Watch the Energy Levels

As we noted from Dan Heath and Chip Heath in Chapter 6, it's natural for change to be exhausting. Expect to wear your virtual seatbelt because there will be potholes and hazards on the road to change success. To even out the ride, monitor personal energy levels throughout the organization, including your own. Principal Evan Robb spoke to this need in our interview: "We solicit feedback from people on the initiatives we're working on to see how effective people believe they are. I also want to get a feel for people's threshold for change—how they respond to the rate of change. Everyone responds to change differently, and what I've found is that a little creative tension in the building is a good thing, but it's not helpful if you're breaking people."

## LEADERSHIP SPOTLIGHT

Look for and celebrate wins. Express thankfulness and appreciation, and honor your journey through celebration.

### The Bottom Line

In short, follow a simple rule: Don't tackle hard stuff when everyone is depleted. Find ways to rest and reenergize as you go.

### Communicate Progress

Share the progress you are making with your stakeholders and your whole staff. This allows them to feel the momentum you've developed around this change initiative and helps them stay aligned with the project. Focus on key victories and learnings. Celebrate interim wins.

Acknowledge progress. Champion thinking and problem solving. Michael Fullan, who has done extensive research in schools around the globe, noted in our conversation that nothing moves the resistors into the action camp as much as success. Former superintendent Karen Rue corroborated this point in our interview.

And once the team has completed the change effort, hold a victory celebration acknowledging everyone's contributions while tying it all back to the larger organizational why.

## A LEADER'S STORY

"We're gonna be okay."

Dr. Karen Rue, former superintendent
Northwest ISD, Texas
Now, Clinical Professor, K–12 Educational Leadership,
Baylor University

I knew we turned the corner of our change initiative when one of our faculty members—who I thought was the curmudgeon of the flagship high school—went down the hall to one of the teachers who was an early adopter and said, "So tell me what you're doing? My kids are talking about that, and they really seem to be enjoying what you're doing down here."

And when he went down the hall to ask about it, I thought, he's one of those informal power brokers, you know. And when he put a seal of approval on something, it was like, you know, the pope had blessed it. And that's when I thought, "Okay, we're gonna be okay. We're gonna make it."

### Transform Change Into the New Standard

Look for ways to institutionalize new activities so they fit into your normal policies and procedures and become easy, repeatable, and expected. Convert key breakthroughs into "how we do things here," integrating the new behaviors into your organizational culture. Superintendent Dave Schuler spoke to this idea in our interview with a simple but bold policy.

## A LEADER'S STORY

"Don't say 'no'!"

Dave Schuler, superintendent, Illinois District 214
2018 Illinois and National Superintendent of the Year
Arlington Heights, Illinois

About eight years ago, I asked our principals and our division heads—and I committed to doing the same thing—not to say "no" when someone wanted to try something new. Unless it's something illegal or immoral, don't say "no." And don't use that word because it just shuts down any possibility for innovation, creativity, curiosity. And so, you can say something like, "Oh, I'm just not sure I'm there yet. Help us get a little bit more information. Help me get to 'yes.'"

The best example is I had an Italian teacher from Prospect, who took a group of kids over to Italy. She came back, and she said, "Dave, I was working with and met with this olive oil owner and manager when I went over there. And they would really like to break into the American market, but they don't know how. What do you think about us working with our career pathways program to see if we can help them break into the U.S. market?"

So, in my head, I'm thinking there's no way this is going to happen, right? But in an e-mail, I got back to her, and I wrote, "Lynn, that is a wonderful idea. Please let me know how I may be of support." And I hit "send." And two years later, our kids are running olive oil kiosks in all of our local malls and at all of our Little Italy festivals. And the [Italian producer] pays for three of our kids to go spend the summer over there learning Italian. And that's because I didn't say "no."

And then we started branching into not saying "no" when growing our career clusters and career pathways program. So now we have sixteen career clusters and forty-four career pathways, and students get to decide what they want to pursue. And we guarantee them an early workplace learning experience.

Keeping these guides in mind during the change phase will help you do the smart work of the focused change successfully and also provide an incredible opportunity to achieve the healthy work of growing the next generation of leaders in your organization.

In our next and final chapter, we'll suggest key positive steps you can take to build on your change effort to make sure that your organizational culture becomes one of curiosity, experimentation, and learning in support of sustained impact toward your organization why.

## Try This

Try your hand at conducting an informal performance acceleration meeting.

### Listen For

- What makes this person tick and how to support their learning and goals.

- Brilliance!—ideas that might support the organization's desired impact.

### Question Options

1. "How are things going?"
2. "What's going well?"
3. "What problems are you encountering?"
4. "What do you think we should do here?"
5. "How can I support you here?"
6. "And what else?"

### Follow-Up

Document any actionable item(s) with time frames. Note who owns any action items.

 Scan this QR code or visit the website at www.shiftingforimpact.com to access the links listed above.

# Creating Sustained Impact 9

Keep moving toward greater impact by creating a culture of ongoing reflection about who you are as a leader, what you are trying to achieve as an organization, and why you must achieve this impact on behalf of the population you serve.

**THE BIG SHIFT**

## Three Steps Underlying Change Success

In Chapter 1, we identified three major reasons why 70 percent of all complex change initiatives fail. Since you've stayed with us to this point, you're motivated to be among the 30 percent that lead successful changes. Great.

To support you, we're going to review and rework those three reasons for change failure to create the positive steps you'll want to take to implement successful change.

### Step 1: Know and Live Your *Why*—Share a Clear, Agreed-Upon Purpose

Purposeful change—the adaptation of the current situation—should be entered into to support your school's or district's why, the outcomes you want to achieve, and the impact you want your organization to have relative to those it serves. On page 140, from our interview, Superintendent Greg Ewing described the circumstances behind his district needing to revisit and champion its why.

## LEADERSHIP SPOTLIGHT

Don't look at change as something that has a beginning and an end. The goal of the leader should be to create a dynamic culture of change in service of the organizational why.

## A LEADER'S STORY

### Responding to a New Reality

Greg Ewing, superintendent
Las Cruces, New Mexico

"At around the same time I went to central office, the demographics of our system started to drastically change. We experienced an influx of migrants coming into the Atlanta area, and all of a sudden, we had ten thousand kids just from Mexico alone appear in the district who couldn't speak English."

Ewing realized that educators would not only have to shift what and how they were doing their work but reconfirm their why if they were to remain impactful relative to the population the district serves.

"When we started, we had a cadre of teachers and leaders who were used to one set of students and one way of teaching, and all of a sudden, they were charged with teaching kids who had limited prior schooling, a lack of English language, a lack of knowledge of U.S. school system policies and procedures. And you had parents who were working enormous numbers of hours and time, so that parental component was not there.

"In the end, we worked for ten years to bring the system to the place where those students were not only being accepted, but the teachers felt comfortable teaching them and were successful doing so."

### Make It Personal

The following questions are intended to help you and your team to explore knowing and living your why:

- Do we have a clear articulation of our why? Has it been shared with everyone? Is it actively used in our work? Visible in our common spaces?

- Do we use simple language to describe our why? Can everyone explain our why? Do they connect the work they do and the efforts they are undertaking to that larger why?

How do we know? How can this connection be made even stronger?

- Are we using this why to challenge the status quo and propel us forward? How can we better align our goals with our why?

- When we have key decisions to make, how might we pause to consider our why during our deliberation so that it informs our decisions? When we communicate new information and key decisions, do we articulate how they align with our why?

- What can we do to intentionally connect to our why as we take action?

## Step 2: Develop and Leverage Your *Who*— Cultivate Leadership Behaviors in Everyone

Change initiatives succeed overwhelmingly not because of smart factors but because of what is known and taken into consideration relative to the people charged with leading and making the change happen. It is the healthy mindset, talents, and behaviors that leaders and staff bring to the task that ultimately determine change success.

Successful organizations will be open to, screen, and adapt the voices of select outside influencers in an effort to self-direct their own change. In short, *they* know and live their why, and *they* determine what they'll need to do to achieve it.

In the "Leader's Story" on the following page, Diane Dugas described her first principalship, where she had to turn around a school facing multiple challenges, including a 70 percent fail rate on state assessments. Her leadership illustrates the power of developing and utilizing both the internal and external who.

### Make It Personal

The following questions are intended to help you and your team evaluate how you're developing and utilizing your who:

- What is our approach to hiring? How do we help new hires fit into our organizational culture and understand our why? How are we ensuring that individuals are operating in alignment with our values and contributing efficiently and

## A LEADER'S STORY

Get the Right People on the Bus

Diane Dugas, director of talent management, EASTCONN
Hampton, Connecticut

The change initiative really entailed understanding our population and what its needs were and then committing to a real social-emotional connection with it. The quality of our staff and their moral compass was critical. In some cases, this situation demanded that there be a turnover in staff. So we had to be able to have those courageous conversations and make those courageous decisions that some people had to go because it wasn't about the adults, it was about the children. So some of the changes involved making new hires—hiring based on satisfying a common vision and mission. Doing so really set the tone in terms of "This is collectively our charge, and you're going to be part of something bigger than just teaching."

We established strong structures around a leadership team that brought in community members, in addition to family members. We looked outside the school. We brought in pastors from the churches and folks from the Rotary as part of our leadership team. Rotary members became mentors and led after-school programs. Church members came in and provided on-site support. We developed a partnership with a community agency tied to a local hospital. We had community policing, so we included members of the police force in our conversations.

I think it's easy for some leaders to put all their attention and focus on those that are the resistors, but if you do that, you never celebrate or move those who can move others. As Michael Fullan says, use the group to move the group. It's not solely up to you as a leader but how you use the group to move others along to build that culture. I think structures like professional learning communities, where people work together and have a voice in decision making, and leadership teams build capacity.

effectively toward our desired outcomes? What process are we using to weed out people who don't fit?

- How well do we know each other? Are there forums for meeting and learning about each other? How strong are our relationships across departments, functions, and levels?

Do we actively encourage connections between people? Can these relationships be leveraged to help people learn and advance in their careers?

- How much of a sense of ownership and autonomy do our people feel? How are we cultivating leadership behavior among staff at all levels? How effectively are we using groups and teams to make decisions and get work accomplished?

- How do we use multiple perspectives to enrich our thinking? What opportunities can we use to engage with and be influenced by our students, their parents, and the communities we serve? How can we intentionally boost diverse voices as we plan and take action? How can we use our next change initiative to drive even more inclusion here?

## Step 3: Strive and Grow Through Your *What*—Act and Reflect to Drive Impact

The what are the shifts you undertake and how you execute them to strive for desired outcomes and impact. Proposed changes are looked at with an eye to what is already working in the organization. Critical here are the frequent and deliberate reflections you make to assess and evaluate progress. In addition, all contemplated shifts should be studied through the lens of coherence rather than as a single event: "How will this change, along with others we've made or are considering, serve our why?" As Figure 9.1 shows (see page 144), changes run parallel to the other work of the school and or district and purposefully follow one another with coherence. Viewed this way, change becomes part of the fabric of the organization's culture.

To increase the likelihood that their change accomplishes its goals, smart and healthy school cultures are not afraid to undertake a high-impact change over an extended period of time and generally eschew flash-in-the-pan, shiny-object panaceas. They create coherence by ensuring a consistent focus. On page 145, Superintendent Dave Schuler, whom we heard from earlier in the book, explains his approach to creating sustained impact.

### Make It Personal

The following questions are intended to help you and your team to consider what you're doing to achieve desired outcomes and impact.

### Figure 9.1   The ARC Model of Change: Working Coherently Toward Your Why

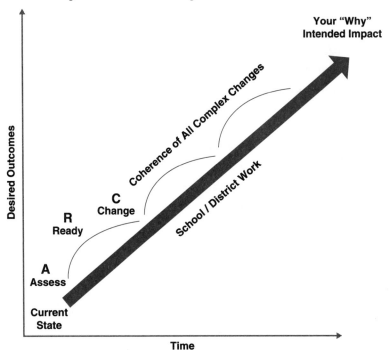

- Do we have a shared sense of accountability? Do we know what we intend to do to make progress toward our why? Can we describe the specific tasks, timelines, and owners for these actions?

- How and how often are we monitoring and measuring progress? How can we link this effort to real-time data on student performance, and how do we adjust instruction accordingly? Do we have frequent "check-in" sessions (for example, weekly or even daily during crunch periods)? Are these check-ins honest, safe, and inspiring? Do we leave them feeling oriented, supported, and energized with a clear sense of what we need to do next to make progress toward our why?

- How is each person regularly held accountable for their assigned tasks? How are we held accountable collectively?

## A LEADER'S STORY

"Take your time."

Dave Schuler, superintendent, Illinois District 214
2018 Illinois and National Superintendent of the Year
Arlington Heights, Illinois

The one thing that I would caution a new administrator about when they consider a complex change is take your time. Think through all the unintended consequences. Rarely, rarely does change need to happen tomorrow. Most beginning superintendents and less seasoned administrators feel like they need to roll up their sleeves and do it tomorrow, and everybody's just going to come with them, and it's going to be awesome. They always say—and I just had this conversation last year with a first-year superintendent, and he said, "But, Dave, how many times is a kid going to be a third grader?" And I said, "Yeah, but how many third-grade classes are you going to have the opportunity to work with to get it right?" Right?

And he did not make it through another year. That role wasn't a good fit for him because he came in wanting to rapidly change the culture of a community, and they weren't interested in having their culture changed. So you could have done it had you stayed five or seven years and having thought through how you were going to put those jigsaw pieces together. We've been working through one change initiative here for the last seven to eight years.

- Do people feel a sense of dissonance or coherence between stated goals, their work, and the change efforts under way? What do we do to address dissonance and enhance coherence?

- How are we deliberately evoking curiosity? What are we experimenting with now, and how are we pausing to reflect and learn from it?

- When are we celebrating our wins? How are we coming together to express gratitude, renew our commitments, and enjoy our community?

## The Reflective Leader

We leave you with a final thought from Mary Howard, who has shared her wisdom a number of times in the book.

"People look at that school and ask, 'Whoa, how did the leader do *that*?' They did it with time; patience; blood, sweat, and tears; hiring the right people; knowing what they wanted to see; and also from ongoing, never-ending professional learning."

So what is the *that* you're working on? Who do you want to impact with it, and why? Who do you want and need standing beside you to accomplish it? What learning along the way will energize you and inform your efforts?

Sustainable success for tomorrow can be started with simple shifts in you today. Carve out a few precious minutes of your day—every day—to pause and reflect. Put a message on your mirror: "How am I helping to achieve the impact we desire?"

> Embrace vulnerability.
>
> Evoke curiosity.
>
> Reward experimentation.
>
> Inspire learning.
>
> Measure progress and adjust.
>
> Lead others to lead.
>
> Lead change differently.

**LEADER VOICES**

**"What future do we envision for our children?"**

Listen to more of the interview we conducted with **Mary Howard**, where she distinguishes between change initiatives and a culture of change. Listen especially for what she means by a collectively embraced *passion-fueled mindset* and the difference between initiatives that are merely an act of "doing" instead of "becoming." (Listen via the QR code on page xiv, or click on Link 9.1 at www.shiftingforimpact.com.)

# References

Adams, S. R. (2005, January 23). *Dilbert* [Cartoon]. Retrieved from https://dilbert.com/strip/2005-01-23

Arnstein, S. R. (1969). A ladder of citizen participation. *Journal of the American Institute of Planners*, *35*(4), 216–224. doi:10.1080/01944366908977225

Boyd, D., & Goldenberg, J. (2013). *Inside the box: A proven system of creativity for breakthrough results*. New York, NY: Simon & Schuster.

Bridges, W., & Bridges, S. M. (2016). *Managing transitions making the most of change* (4th ed.). Boston, MA: Da Capo Lifelong Books.

Bungay Stanier, M. (2016). *The coaching habit*. Toronto, Canada: Box of Crayons Press.

Bunting, M. (2016). *The mindful leader: 7 practices for transforming your leadership, your organization and your life*. Milton, Australia: John Wiley and Sons Australia.

Cashman, K. (1998). *Leadership from the inside out: Becoming a leader for life*. Provo, UT: Executive Excellence Publishing.

Cashman, K. (2012). *The pause principle*. San Francisco, CA: Berrett-Koehler.

Certo, S. C., & Certo, S. T. (2019). *Modern management: Concepts and skills*. New York, NY: Pearson.

Collins, J. C. (2001). *Good to great: Why some companies make the leap . . . and others don't* (1st ed.). New York: Harper Business.

Collins, J. C. (2005). *Good to great and the social sectors: Why business thinking is not the answer*. New York, NY: HarperCollins.

Collins, J. C. (2019). *Turning the flywheel*. New York, NY: HarperCollins.

Davis, K. (2018). *Brave leadership: Unleash your most confident, powerful, and authentic self to get the results you need*. Austin, TX: Greenleaf Book Group Press.

Duhigg, C. (2016, February 28). What Google learned from its quest to build the perfect team. *New York Times Magazine*. Retrieved from https://www.nytimes.com/2016/02/28/magazine/what-google-learned-from-its-quest-to-build-the-perfect-team.html?ref=magazine

Friedman, T. L. (2016). *Thank you for being late: An optimist's guide to thriving in the age of accelerations*. New York, NY: Farrar, Straus and Giroux.

Fullan, M., & Quinn, J. (2016). *Coherence: The right drivers in action for schools, districts, and systems*. Thousand Oaks, CA: Corwin.

George, B. (2003). *Authentic leadership: Rediscovering the secrets to creating lasting value*. San Francisco, CA: Jossey-Bass.

George, B. (2015). *Discover your true north*. Hoboken, NJ: Wiley.

Goffee, R., & Jones, G. (2000, September/October). Why should anyone be led by you? *Harvard Business Review*.

Goleman, D. (2018) The secret behind authentic leadership. *Korn Ferry Reports & Insights*. Retrieved from https://www.kornferry.com/institute/authentic-leadership-emotional-intelligence

Goleman, D., Boyatzis, R. E., & McKee, A. (2001, December). Primal leadership: The hidden driver of great performance. *Harvard Business Review.*

Goleman, D., Boyatzis, R., & McKee, A. (2002). *Primal leadership: Realizing the power of emotional intelligence.* Boston, MA: Harvard Business Review Press.

Gray, S. P., & Streshly, W. A. (2008). *From good schools to great schools: What their principals do well.* Thousand Oaks, CA: Corwin Press.

Heath, D., & Heath, C. (2010). *Switch: How to change things when change is hard.* New York, NY: Broadway Books.

Hecht, D. (2013). The neural basis of optimism and pessimism. *Experimental Neurobiology, 22*(3), 173–199. doi:10.5607/en.2013.22.3.173

Hedges, K. (2014, September 23). If you think leadership development is a waste of time you may be right. *ForbesWomen*. Retrieved from https://www.forbes.com/sites/work-in-progress/2014/09/23/if-you-think-leadership-development-is-a-waste-of-time-you-may-be-right/#5d158a035bf4

Hughes, M. (2019, May 3). The secret sauce of employee engagement [Video log post]. Retrieved from https://www.youtube.com/watch?time_continue=124&v=n0TAbJYPj1I

Kapila, M., Hines, E., & Searby, M. (2016, Fall). Why diversity, equity, and inclusion matter. *Independent Sector*, 10–16. Retrieved from https://independentsector.org/resource/why-diversity-equity-and-inclusion-matter

Kegan, R., & Lahey, L. L. (2001). *How the way we talk can change the way we work: Seven languages for transformation.* Hoboken, NJ: John Wiley & Sons.

Kegan, R., & Lahey, L. L. (2009). *Immunity to change: How to overcome it and unlock the potential in yourself and your organization.* Boston, MA: Harvard Business Review Press.

Kim, J., & Bang, S. C. (2013, Spring). What are the top cultural characteristics that appear in high-performing organizations across multiple industries? Retrieved from https://digitalcommons.ilr.cornell.edu/student/38/

Kirtman, L., & Fullan, M. (2016). *Leadership: Key competencies for whole-system change.* Bloomington, IN: Solution Tree Press.

Lencioni, P. (2012). *The advantage: Why organizational health trumps everything else in business.* San Francisco, CA: Jossey-Bass.

Leonard, D., & Coltea, C. (2013, March 24). Most change initiatives fail—but they don't have to. *Gallup Business Journal.* Retrieved from https://news.gallup.com/businessjournal/162707/change-initiatives-fail-don.aspx

Marquet, L. D. (2013). *Turn the ship around!: A true story of building leaders by breaking the rules.* London, UK: Portfolio Penguin.

Mathis, T. (2015, August 12). What is human systems integration? [Web log post]. Retrieved from http://blog.apabooks.org/2015/08/12/what-is-human-systems-integraton

McKee, A., & Boyatzis, R. (2005). *Resonant leadership: Renewing yourself and connecting with others through mindfulness, hope, and compassion.* Boston, MA: Harvard Business School Press.

Moesby, E. (2004). Reflections on making a change towards project oriented and problem-based learning (POPBL). *World Transactions on Engineering and Technology Education, 3*(2), 269–278. Retrieved from http://www.wiete.com.au/journals/WTE&TE/Pages/Vol.3,No.2(2004)/20_Moesby24.pdf

Niche.com Inc. (2018, March 07). Explore Wethersfield School District. Retrieved August 20, 2019, from https://www.niche.com/k12/d/wethersfield-school-district-ct/#reviews

Pressfield, S. (2012). *The war of art break through the blocks and win your inner creative battles.* New York, NY: Black Irish Entertainment.

Racial Equity Tools. (n.d.). Racial equity tools glossary. Retrieved from https://www.racialequitytools.org/glossary#about-text

Royal Society for the Encouragement of Arts, Manufactures, and Commerce. (2010, October 14). RSA ANIMATE: Changing education paradigms. Retrieved from https://www.youtube.com/watch?v=zDZFcDGpL4U

Schwantes, M. (2017, November 22). Research: Why 70 percent of employees aren't working to their full potential comes down to 1 simple reason. Retrieved August 20, 2019, from https://www.inc.com/marcel-schwantes/research-why-70-percent-of-employees-arent-working-to-their-full-potential-comes-down-to-1-simple-reason.html

Shannon, G. S., & Byslma, P. (2007, June). *Nine characteristics of high-performing schools: A research-based resource for schools and districts to assist with improving student learning. Second edition.* Retrieved from https://eric.ed.gov/?id=ED499819

Sinek, S. (2009). *Start with why: How great leaders inspire everyone to take action.* New York, NY: Portfolio.

TEDx Talks. (2013, June 20). Know your inner saboteurs: Shirzad Chamine at TEDxStanford. Retrieved from https://www.youtube.com/watch?v=-zdJ1ubvoXs

Ury, W. (2016, Summer). Go to the balcony. *Dawson Magazine,* 8–11. Retrieved from https://dawsonschool.myschoolapp.com/ftpimages/715/download/download_2173811.pdf

Whitmore, J. (2009). *Coaching for performance: Growing human potential and purpose* (4th ed.). Boston, MA: Nicholas Brealey.

Wiggins, G. P., & McTighe, J. (2005). *Understanding by design.* Alexandria, VA: Association for Supervision and Curriculum Development.

Wiseman, L., Allen, L., & Foster, E. (2013). *The multiplier effect: Tapping the genius inside our schools.* Thousand Oaks, CA: Corwin.

# Index

A SAGE Publishing Company

**CORWIN HAS ONE MISSION:** to enhance education through intentional professional learning.

We build long-term relationships with our authors, educators, clients, and associations who partner with us to develop and continuously improve the best evidence-based practices that establish and support lifelong learning.

# *Leadership* That Makes an Impact

**MICHAEL FULLAN & MARY JEAN GALLAGHER**

With the goal of transforming the culture of learning to develop greater equity, excellence, and student well-being, this book will help you liberate the system and maintain focus.

**PETER M. DEWITT**

This step-by-step how-to guide presents the six driving forces of instructional leadership within a multistage model for implementation, delivering lasting improvement through small collaborative changes.

**BRYAN GOODWIN**

If you've ever wondered anything, really—just out of curiosity—then you have what it takes to lead your school to restored curiosity and your students to well-being and success.

**JOHN HATTIE & RAYMOND L. SMITH**

Based on the most current Visible Learning® research with contributions from education thought leaders around the world, this book includes practical ideas for leaders to implement high-impact strategies to strengthen entire school cultures and advocate for all students.

**DAVIS CAMPBELL & MICHAEL FULLAN**

The model outlined in this book develops a systems approach to governing local schools collaboratively to become exemplars of highly effective decision-making, leadership, and action.

**MICHAEL FULLAN, JOANNE QUINN, & JOANNE MCEACHEN**

The comprehensive strategy of deep learning incorporates practical tools and processes to engage educational stakeholders in new partnerships, mobilize whole-system change, and transform learning for all students.

**JOANNE QUINN, JOANNE MCEACHEN, MICHAEL FULLAN, MAG GARDNER, & MAX DRUMMY**

Dive into deep learning with this hands-on guide to creating learning experiences that give purpose, unleash student potential, and transform not only learning, but life itself.

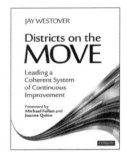

**JAY WESTOVER**

The transformative framework outlined in this book creates a districtwide approach for changing the culture of learning and creating a coherent system of continuous improvement.

**ANTHONY KIM, KEARA MASCARENAZ, & KAWAI LAI**

This guide provides battle-tested practices to help leaders build better habits for team learning, meetings, and projects, to achieve a more responsive, innovative organization.

**EVAN ROBB**

Build the foundations of effective leadership despite daily distractions. Learn how to intentionally use ten-minute opportunities to consider and execute your vision.

**AMY TEPPER & PATRICK FLYNN**

Nineteen strategies help leaders, coaches, and teachers improve their ability to identify desired outcomes, recognize learning in action, collect relevant evidence, and develop effective feedback.

**JULIE M. WILSON**

Learn to make sense of challenging change journeys and accelerate implementation with this practical framework that includes human-centered tools, resources, and mini case studies.

**GRANT LICHTMAN**

Our rapidly evolving world is dramatically impacting how we view schools. *Thrive* shows educators how they can help their schools not only survive but thrive during rapid change.

**ERIC SHENINGER**

The future-forward framework in this book prepares leaders to harness the power of innovative ideas and digital strategies to create relevant, engaging, and intuitive school cultures.

**CHRISTINE MASON, PAUL LIABENOW, & MELISSA PATSCHKE**

Envision and enact transformative change with an iterative visioning process, thought-provoking vignettes, case studies from exemplary schools, key strategies and tools, and practical implementation ideas.

**KIRSTEN RICHERT, JEFFREY IKLER, & MARGARET ZACCHEI**

*Shifting* empowers educational change leaders to proactively and coherently navigate complex, unprecedented change in schools and establish a school culture in which changemakers can thrive.